Mental Math
in the Primary Grades

Jack A. Hope • Larry Leutzinger • Barbara J. Reys • Robert E. Reys

DALE SEYMOUR PUBLICATIONS

Cover design: Rachel Gage
Illustrations: Mitchell Rose

Order number DS01814
ISBN 0-86651-434-1

DALE
SEYMOUR
PUBLICATIONS
P.O. BOX 10888
PALO ALTO, CA 94303

fghijk-MA-9543210

CONTENTS

PREFACE

Learning to calculate mentally, without the use of external memory aids (including paper and pencil), has many benefits.

1. **Calculating in your head is a practical life skill.** Many types of everyday computation problems can be solved mentally. In fact, practically speaking, many *must* be solved mentally, since we often need to make quick computations when we don't have a calculator or paper and pencil at hand. For example: You are at the airport. The departure board indicates that your flight is scheduled to leave at 3:35. Your watch shows that it's now 2:49. How much time do you have? Enough time to grab a snack? Here's another example: You find tuna fish on sale at the supermarket for 69 cents a can. You would like to stock up now, but you know that you have only $10 with you, and you also need to buy bread and milk. How many cans of tuna could you buy on sale? These and similar situations demonstrate the everyday utility of mental math skills.

2. **Skill at mental math can make written computation easier or quicker.** A student who is dependent on written algorithms might calculate 1000×945 this way:

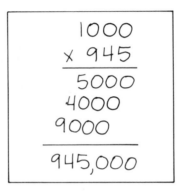

Knowing how to "tack on trailing zeros," a mental math skill, can reduce that process to one step: **$1000 \times 945 = 945{,}000$.** Similarly, faced with the addition of long columns of figures, even with a pencil in hand, the mental math skill "searching for compatible pairs" can simplify the computation. For example, finding numbers that sum to ten makes this addition quicker than taking it step by step:

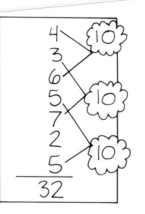

In these and many other ways, mental math skills can streamline students' written work and increase their understanding at the same time.

3. **Proficiency in mental math contributes to increased skill in estimation.** Estimation has come to be recognized as an important part of the mathematics curriculum. It is essential for checking the reasonableness of an answer obtained through the use of a calculator, and estimation skills are useful in solving many everyday problems as well. Mental calculation provides the cornerstone for all estimation processes, offering a variety of alternative algorithms and nonstandard techniques for finding answers.

4. **Mental calculation can lead to a better understanding of place value, mathematical operations, and basic number properties.** Students often do written computation mechanically, without a great deal of thought, simply applying the written algorithms with very little sense of what they are *really* doing. Efficient paper-and-pencil calculation demands careful attention to digits and bookkeeping rules and contributes to a fragmentary view of number relationships. Mental computation, on the other hand, forces students to think about numbers and number relationships. As students learn to manipulate numbers in their heads, they develop a keen number sense and experience increased confidence in their mathematical abilities. Such confidence ensures that these students will not have to turn to a machine or pencil and paper for every straightforward calculation they encounter in daily life.

Despite its many attractive benefits, mental calculation has not played a prominent role in most contemporary mathematics programs. Because of this neglect, most people are not very proficient mental calculators. Recent studies have demonstrated that a large majority of children and young adults cannot perform even the simplest mental calculations. For example, the third National Assessment of Educational Progress in mathematics found that less than half of the 13-year-old sample correctly calculated the product of 60 and 70 "in the head" within 9 seconds. According to the same survey, most children were unaware that a mental calculation is often the most convenient method of solution. For example, only 38 percent of the 13-year-olds thought that the exercise 945×1000 should be done mentally; the majority claimed that either a pencil and paper or a calculator was needed to determine the solution.

Undoubtedly, this performance reflects the current lack of attention given to mental computation by textbook publishers and curriculum developers. To counter this we offer the *Mental Math* series, a planned program of instruction in mental calculation that complements any current elementary school mathematics program. We think you will find the lessons fun and easy to teach. Used regularly, with plenty of practice, these materials can turn your whole class into "mentalmathletes."

Jack Hope
Larry Leutzinger
Barbara Reys
Robert Reys

INTRODUCTION

Teaching Primary Mathematics

As primary grade teachers, we have many priorities and objectives for our students as they progress through the early mathematics curriculum. These objectives include the learning of basic facts as well as standard paper-and-pencil computational procedures. Instruction dealing with each of these areas must include an emphasis on *teaching for understanding*. In particular, we must not limit instruction in computation to paper-and-pencil techniques, because that gives students the impression that such procedures (written algorithms) are necessary to compute *all* arithmetic problems. This result is especially unfortunate when we consider how often we as adults use mental algorithms to compute practical, everyday problems.

Recently, professional groups such as the National Council of Teachers of Mathematics Standards Committee have encouraged a careful examination of the computation strand of the mathematics curriculum at all grade levels, including primary. They recommend attention to various methods of computation, including mental, paper-and-pencil, calculator, and approximate computation. They also advise us to take a conceptual approach to teaching computation with careful attention to the underlying concepts, using physical materials as models and developing good *thinking* strategies.

As we work to help our young students develop quick recall of basic facts, we need also to help them develop an awareness of when they can use these facts with *mental* strategies to compute problems that involve larger numbers. For example, primary students ought to realize that a problem such as 40 + 50 is simply an extension of a basic fact (4 + 5) and thus be able to find the answer without using a paper-and-pencil algorithm. In our experience, specific teaching of such mental strategies has to be included in the curriculum. Without it, students who have been advised at a young age to "show your work" or "write it all down" will routinely follow rote procedures that were meant for paper-and-pencil computation, even when mental algorithms might be more appropriate (as when computing problems such as 24 + 10 or 240 + 250).

With this book, you can lead your students to an understanding of what mental computation is and what thinking processes underlie it.

About the *Mental Math* Series

Mental Math in the Primary Grades is the first in a series of three books designed to help teach students in grades one through eight the techniques of "figuring in your head." This book, suited for students in grades one through three, focuses on simple calculation with whole numbers with an emphasis on the operations of addition and subtraction. Lessons in the first two units present good reasoning strategies to help students learn and remember the basic facts of addition and subtraction. The last two units present easy methods for adding and subtracting mentally with tens and hundreds (easily extended to thousands). In addition, a variety of physical models are used to highlight important place value patterns in the base ten number system.

The second book in the series, *Mental Math in the Middle Grades* (grades four through six), extends the skills developed in the primary book to more difficult mental calculations with whole numbers. The third book, *Mental Math in Junior High* (grades six through eight), contains more advanced lessons that introduce methods of calculating mentally with fractions, decimals, and percents, as well as whole numbers.

Features of This Book

Mental Math in the Primary Grades contains 36 lessons in mental mathematics. The book is divided into four units:

Unit One: Thinking Strategies for Addition
Unit Two: Thinking Strategies for Subtraction
Unit Three: Thinking in Patterns
Unit Four: Thinking Strategies for Larger Numbers

Each unit opens with an overview that establishes the objectives and rationale for the lessons that follow. This overview includes an idea for a bulletin board display that will support the unit's lessons.

A unit contains nine lessons, each lesson consisting of two pages: first, a page of *teaching notes* that describe the lesson and offer suggestions for extension and follow-up, backed by a *teaching transparency* in the form of a blackline master that you can reproduce on acetate for use with an overhead projector as you present the lesson. At the close of each unit is a short progress test, designed to be given orally. Reproducible pages at the end of the book include "Power Builder" practice sets for some of the lessons, 100 charts in two sizes, and a master for creating base ten blocks out of tagboard when other models are not available.

Teaching Mental Math

SCHEDULING AND PLANNING THE LESSONS

If you want to cover all the material in this book in a single school year, the 36 lessons allow for a pace of one lesson per week. However, you will likely want to choose lessons appropriate to your students and concentrate groups of lessons around similar content you are teaching. For example, since all nine lessons in Unit One focus on addition of basic facts, you might use these lessons while you are developing this content in your curriculum. Similarly, use lessons from Unit Two to focus on subtraction of basic facts, lessons from Unit Three as you deal with place value, and lessons from Unit Four to present simple techniques for mentally calculating with multidigit numbers.

PRESENTING THE LESSONS

Each of the lessons can generally be presented within 10–15 minutes, and therefore would make a good "warm-up" for your math period. Before teaching a lesson, familiarize yourself with the general approach by reading the teaching notes. These notes include the following sections:

ABOUT THE LESSON Important background and rationale for the lesson.

YOU WILL NEED ... Materials used in presenting the lesson.

TEACHING THE LESSON Detailed, step-by-step instructions for carrying out the lesson, using the corresponding transparency and other relevant materials. This section includes answers for the "TRY THESE" exercises that appear at the bottom of the teaching transparencies in Unit Four. TRY THESE exercises are designed as guided practice to reinforce the lesson content, giving students a chance to apply the new strategy and allowing you to see how well they have understood it.

EXTENDING THE LESSON Ideas for activities that are a bit more advanced than those presented in the lesson. You might turn to this section a few days after presenting the initial lesson, particularly when a class has caught on to the new technique very quickly. Or, you might use this section with a small group of students who are ready for a more advanced application of the technique.

ORAL FOLLOW-UP Oral presentation of questions and problems generally of the same type and difficulty level as those in the main lesson. You might use this oral follow-up the day after presenting the lesson to review the content in a different presentation mode.

After familiarizing yourself with the teaching notes, gather the necessary materials and use the blackline master to make the transparency for the lesson.

As you teach each new lesson, be sure to spend time developing and *discussing* the concept presented. This discussion should continue throughout the sample problems suggested in the lesson. At this stage you are not working on *speed* in mental calculation; you are working on *understanding*. With each problem, pause to discuss the students' responses and ask them to explain the thinking strategies they used.

As you will discover, class discussion is a critical part of teaching mental math because there is no other way for students to "show their work." It's all taking place in their heads, and talking about students' thought processes is the only way to find out how well they understand the strategies.

PRACTICING THE STRATEGIES

Use the suggested follow-up activities ("Extending the Lesson" and "Oral Follow-Up") to give students the practice they will need to become proficient at mental math. When appropriate, use the corresponding Power Builder, a reproducible page of exercises for independent practice.

As you move from group discussion to independent work, continue to insist that students do the problems *mentally*. When working on the Power Builders, students will need pencils to record their answers, but that is *all* the pencils should be used for. You may want to circulate around the classroom to remind students of the "in your head" rule while they are working on the practice sets.

For the Power Builders for Units One and Two, specific timing instructions are given in the unit overviews. In these first units dealing with the basic facts, students should first practice the *strategy* involved in the lesson, then practice specific combinations related to that strategy. Practicing the strategy for mastery should require only a few days for 5 minutes each day; practicing and drilling the combinations for mastery will take much longer. However, learning the basic facts through the use of these thinking strategies will be easier and faster than by any other method.

When using the Power Builders in Unit Four, you might set a target time limit of 3 minutes. This allows about 10 seconds per problem. Feel free to adjust this time to the difficulty of the problems and the abilities of your students. The best timing standards can be determined by experimenting with your class.

USING THE TESTS

Four short oral progress tests are provided, one at the end of each unit. Students use a blank sheet of lined paper to record their answers. Use these tests to provide a review and wrap-up of the ideas presented in the unit. You may want to use each as both a pre- and post-test. If so, simply administer the unit test just *before* presenting the unit's lessons and then again *afterwards* to assess student growth.

Thinking Strategies for Addition

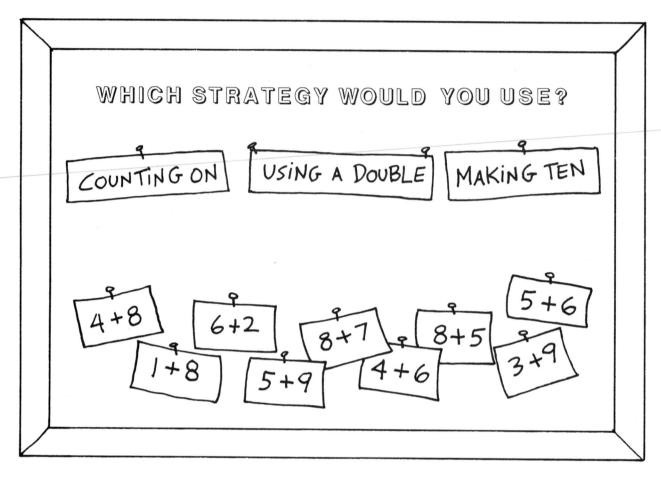

UNIT ONE OVERVIEW

Most primary teachers agree that eventually students should know all the basic addition and subtraction facts. *How* they should learn these facts is a matter for debate. An increasing body of research indicates that teaching students specific "thinking strategies" not only increases the likelihood that they will learn the basic facts, but also provides them with a framework of mental strategies on which more advanced thinking techniques can be built.

In this unit, students will encounter three basic thinking strategies that can help them master the basic addition facts. These strategies are *counting on, using a double,* and *adding to make ten.* The strategy of counting on is useful for learning the facts in which one of the addends is 1, 2, or 3 (for example, 6 + 2, 3 + 9, 1 + 8). Using a double is helpful when one of the addends is just 1 or 2 more than the other (as in 4 + 6, 8 + 7, 5 + 6). Adding to make ten is especially useful when one of the addends is 8 or 9 (as in 4 + 8, 5 + 9, 8 + 5).

When using a mental math or "thinking" strategy to teach basic facts, the best approach is first to model the strategy with concrete or visual materials, then to provide practice in the strategy using those same materials (counters, dot patterns, ten-frames, hundreds squares, and so forth). The goal of this practice is to develop the thinking strategy independent of any particular basic facts. Once the students can quickly and accurately use the strategy with the concrete or visual models, they are ready to apply the strategy to specific combinations. You can then present appropriate addition combinations expressed symbolically.

BULLETIN BOARD FOR UNIT ONE

As students learn to apply thinking strategies to the basic addition facts, they must be able to identify which thinking strategy is most useful in determining the answer to a particular combination. A bulletin board display like the one shown opposite offers students the chance to classify addition combinations by strategies.

Write the various addition combinations on index cards and tack them randomly to the board. Include at least 10 combinations appropriate for each strategy. Students place the cards under an appropriate strategy sign. Later have the students write 5 of their own cards for each strategy.

Note that some combinations might be classified under more than one strategy. For instance, 9 + 8 could be thought of as a case for making ten (9 + 1 + 7); it might also be solved by using a double (8 + 8 + 1). Students need to understand that either strategy is appropriate. This is an idea basic to the *Mental Math* program: that there is no single "right" way to do a problem in your head. Students need to be flexible as they learn alternative strategies. Ultimately, they should be encouraged to use whichever method works best for them.

WORKING FOR MASTERY

Give students all the time they need to learn about using the strategy with addition combinations. Delay any drill on those combinations until students are comfortable with the strategy and can find sums quickly. At that point, drill is in order. Each drill should be of short duration, with feedback provided immediately. For example, after you state an addition combination, you might give the students 5 seconds to write the answer. After 5 seconds, you would state the correct answer and go on to the next combination. You might repeat this procedure for 10 combinations. As the students become familiar with your drill format, you can cut the time between stating the combination and giving the answer. Set 2 seconds as a goal. If you hold a short session of drill daily, you should see students' speed increasing dramatically in as little as two weeks. For evaluation purposes, follow the same basic procedure but do not give the answers.

Five reproducible Power Builder pages are provided to help students develop mastery of the thinking strategies in Unit One and the basic addition facts. The first three Power Builders, designed for follow-up practice after specific lessons in the unit, contain four rows with eight combinations in each row. Allow the students 50 seconds to do the first row, 40 seconds to do the second, 30 to do the third, and 20 to do the fourth. Requiring the students to answer quickly is *very* important because that is the only way to ensure that they are using an efficient mental strategy to determine the answer. The next two Power Builders are a collection of the relevant basic addition facts, for use as timed mental practice sheets after you have completed all of Unit One.

Lesson 1   Counting On

ABOUT THE LESSON

Counting on is an important skill for students to learn because it is involved in addition, numeration, counting money, and telling time. This lesson presents carefully structured activities with various concrete models to help develop this skill. You will ask the students to start from a number less than 10 and count on 1, 2, or 3. You can also extend the activities to work with numbers larger than 10.

YOU WILL NEED . . .
- Counters
- Styrofoam cup
- Number cards for 5, 6, 7, 8, 9, 10, 11, and 12 *(Use whatever cards you may have, or simply write the numbers on small oak tag squares or index cards.)*
- Gum in packets of 5, 6, 7, and 8 pieces
- Transparency 1, "Counting On"

TEACHING THE LESSON

Place 5 counters in the cup and set the number card for 5 next to it, explaining that the 5 on the card tells how many counters are inside. As the students watch, drop 2 more counters (one at a time) into the cup. Ask the students to write the number of counters contained in the cup now. Tell them to "count on," starting with 5 and counting on from there to find the total number. Demonstrate by saying, "five [softly] . . . SIX, SEVEN." Have a student tell which number card should now be placed next to the cup. Check by counting all the counters.

Repeat for other numbers, dropping 1, 2, or 3 additional counters into the cup each time.

Show a packet of gum containing 5 sticks and 2 additional loose sticks. Have students write how many sticks there are in all. Count on with them *(five [softly] . . . SIX, SEVEN)* to check the answer. Repeat, using packets of 6, 7, and 8 pieces with 1, 2, or 3 additional loose sticks.

Place Transparency 1 on the overhead. With an overhead pen, write 7 in the box beside the pocket. Tell the following story:

Kristin had 7 acorns in her pocket. She found two more acorns in the grass and put them into her pocket, too. How many acorns does she have in her pocket now?

Have students write the answer. Encourage them to count on to determine the total.

Write 8 in the box beside the piggy bank and tell this story:

Leona had 8 pennies in her bank. Her mother gave her 3 more pennies for picking up her room. How many pennies does Leona have in her bank now? (Have students write the answer.)

Write 12 beside the cookie jar and tell this story:

Heath's mother baked some oatmeal cookies for him to take to school. She had 12 cookies left over, and she put them in the cookie jar. When Heath came home from school, he brought 1 cookie back and put it in the jar with the others. How many cookies are in the jar now? (Have students write the answer.)

Repeat the activities with different numbers and different stories.

EXTENDING THE LESSON

Have individual students select any of the pictures on the transparency and write any number in the box. The student must then tell a story and ask a question that fits the situation. Other class members should determine the answer, but the student must know the answer to the question he or she asks.

ORAL FOLLOW-UP

Read the following story problems. Encourage students to count on to find the answers.

- Imagine a doghouse with 6 dogs in it. Three more dogs come. How many dogs are in the doghouse now? (9 dogs)

- Think about 7 cars in a parking lot. Two more cars drive into the lot. How many cars are in the lot now? (9 cars)

- Marty had 9 pennies in a coin purse. While walking to school, he saw another penny on the sidewalk. He picked it up and put it into the purse. Now how many coins does he have in the purse? (10 coins)

- Emily put 12 blocks together to form a train. Her brother added 3 blocks. How many blocks are there in all? (15 blocks)

- As Tracey left school, she was carrying 5 library books. Justin asked Tracey to hold both of his books while he tied his shoe. How many books was Tracey holding while Justin tied his shoe? (7 books)

Make up other story problems that involve counting on 1, 2, or 3.

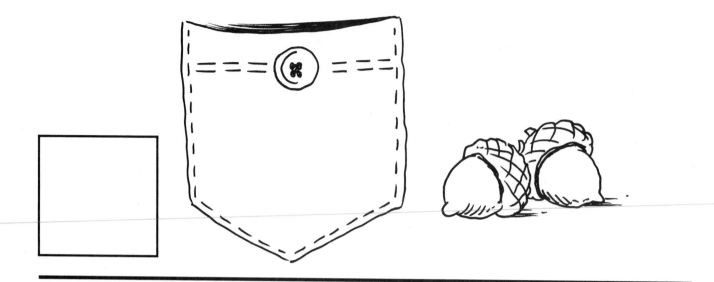

Lesson 2 More Counting On

ABOUT THE LESSON
Lesson 1 presented counting on 1, 2, or 3 through concrete and representational examples. This lesson expands on that strategy, applying it now to addition combinations that are stated symbolically. For example, for the combination 2 + 7, the students are directed to start with the larger number and count on the amount of the smaller number *(seven . . . EIGHT, NINE)*. Multiple-step problems involving counting on are presented as an extension.

YOU WILL NEED . . .
- Number cards for 4, 5, 6, 7, 8, and 9
- Counters
- Transparency 2, "Add by Counting On"
- Power Builder 1, page 89

TEACHING THE LESSON
Hold up the number card for 7. Take 2 counters in your other hand and show them to the group. Tell the students to pretend that there are 7 counters behind the number card. Ask, "How many counters in all?" Then ask what addition fact was just shown. (7 + 2 = 9) Repeat this activity using other cards and 1, 2, or 3 counters.

Ask a student to hold up a card and counters to show the combination 8 + 3. Tell the class to count on to find the total. Have another student state the complete addition fact. (8 + 3 = 11) Repeat for other combinations.

Place Transparency 2 on the overhead, covering the bottom half to focus attention on the first number line. Show the frog and the cricket (the students might name them), and tell this story:

These two friends like to add by jumping along a number line. The frog, who takes BIG hops, always jumps to the larger number in an addition combination. Then the little cricket, who jumps only one space at a time, jumps on from where the frog landed.

Point to the first combination, 2 + 6, and demonstrate by moving the characters along the line as you explain:

To add these numbers, the frog would jump to the 6 . . . and the cricket would make 2 more hops . . . to the 7 and then to the 8.

Have students show how the two friends would jump to add 3 + 7 and 8 + 2. Continue with other combinations involving 1, 2, or 3.

Now show the second number line and have students continue jumping the frog and cricket to add the combinations shown. Emphasize begin-ning with the greater number, then counting on the amount of the lesser number. When students seem to be comfortable with this strategy, put aside the frog and cricket and work with just the number lines. For each addition combination you give, you might have a student circle the greater number, then count on.

EXTENDING THE LESSON
Present counting-on combinations using the language of addition. Include larger numbers, but count on only 1, 2, or 3. For example:

What is 2 more than 9? (11)

What is 10 plus 3? (13) Write an addition fact using those numbers. (10 + 3 = 13)

What number is 1 greater than 42? (43) Write an addition fact. (42 + 1 = 43)

What is the sum of 64 and 2? (66)

If one *part* is 8 and the other *part* is 2, what is the *total*? (10) *[The wording of this last example—part, part, and total—is important and will be emphasized in later lessons.]*

Repeat for other combinations. Ask the students not only to determine the answer but also to write the resulting addition fact.

ORAL FOLLOW-UP
Present story problems that involve counting on 1, 2, or 3. To make them more difficult, include two steps. For example:

- Raoul had a stamp collection with 45 stamps in it. His father gave him 2 more stamps and his mother gave him 3 more. How many stamps did Raoul have then? (50 stamps)

- Kenny traded a colored pencil for 2 marbles. He then traded his favorite seashell for a big marble. If Kenny started with 15 marbles, how many did he have after his trades? (18 marbles)

- Portia counted 36 blackbirds on a wire. After she finished counting, 1 bird joined them, then 3 more came. Portia started to count all the birds again. Can you tell Portia how many birds are on the wire? (40 birds)

- Darrell was selling lemonade for 5¢ a glass. By noon, he had sold 17 glasses. Then the woman next door bought 1 glass for herself, 1 for her husband, and 3 for their children. How many glasses had Darrell sold then? How much money did he take in altogether? (22 glasses, $1.10)

INDIVIDUAL PRACTICE
Distribute copies of Power Builder 1 for more practice in counting on 1, 2, or 3.

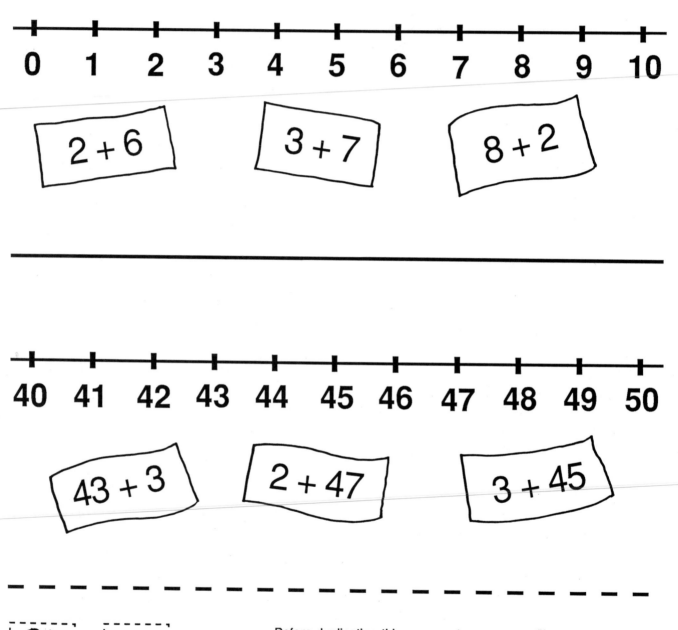

0 1 2 3 4 5 6 7 8 9 10

2 + 6   3 + 7   8 + 2

40 41 42 43 44 45 46 47 48 49 50

43 + 3   2 + 47   3 + 45

Before duplicating this page on transparency film, cut off the bottom section along the dotted line. Reproduce the frog and cricket on a separate transparency, color as desired, and cut out on dotted lines for use with the number lines above.

Lesson 3   Doubling Numbers

ABOUT THE LESSON

Many students learn doubles before any other fact combinations, so this lesson offers them a chance to practice a basic skill that they may already know. Being able to double numbers mentally will be useful in mental math strategies throughout the grades. At the primary grades, students can use this skill to learn related addition facts (as will be presented in lesson 5). The ability to double a number will also be useful for certain multiplication facts and more sophisticated mental math strategies (as presented in *Mental Math in the Middle Grades*).

For this lesson, the goal is for students to be able to name, quickly and accurately, the double of any number from 1 to 9. Dot pictures set up in double frames (similar to dominoes, but based on the more familiar dot patterns found on dice) give students a way to visualize the combinations in their minds.

YOU WILL NEED . . .
• Transparency 3, "Doubles"

TEACHING THE LESSON

Place Transparency 3 on the overhead. Cover the bottom part of each double-frame dot picture with a small card. Point to the top half of the first picture (4 + 4) and tell the students to name the total if we double the 4 dots. Expose the bottom half and let them check their answers by counting the total. Encourage them to use an efficient counting strategy, such as counting on from the first addend. Repeat this procedure for each dot picture.

Remove the transparency and place a few objects (counters, paper clips, or the like) on the screen. Use any number of objects from 1 to 9. Ask students to determine the total if we double this number of objects. Then ask them to write an addition fact for each situation.

Have the students write the answers to the following addition exercises (stated orally):

3 + 3 (6)	5 + 5 (10)
7 + 7 (14)	4 + 4 (8)
9 + 9 (18)	2 + 2 (4)
6 + 6 (12)	8 + 8 (16)

Repeat these in a different order.

EXTENDING THE LESSON

1. Say the following numbers and have the students double each: 10, 12, 14, 15, 20, 22, 31, 41. Have the students double other numbers as well. Select two-digit numbers with neither digit larger than 5.

2. Ask students to write the number that, when doubled, gives an answer of 16; 12; 10; 18; 14; 6; 8.

3. Ask students to double multiples of 10: double 20, double 40, double 10, double 30, double 60, double 70, double 50, double 80, double 90.

ORAL FOLLOW-UP

Ask the following questions:
• How many legs do 2 dogs have? (8 legs)
• Two tricycles have how many wheels? (6 wheels)
• One pencil costs 9 cents. How much do 2 pencils cost? (18 cents)
• Barry and Harry are twins. Their mother always dresses them alike. One day the boys each had on a shirt with 7 buttons. How many buttons were there on both shirts? (14 buttons)
• Two octopuses have how many legs? (16 legs)
• If one box holds 5 toy cars, how many cars do you get in 2 boxes? (10 cars)
• Nancy rolled 2 sixes on the dice. What was the total? (12)

Make up other word problems that involve doubles.

Lesson 4   Doubling Doubles

ABOUT THE LESSON
Students should be proficient with doubles (lesson 3) before working with this lesson, in which they practice doubling numbers that are themselves doubles. A 10-by-10 array is used to present the doubles, giving students a visual model to use in their thinking. Many of this lesson's activities have natural extensions to teaching strategies for multiplication facts.

YOU WILL NEED . . .
• Transparency 4, "Doubling Doubles"

TEACHING THE LESSON
Place Transparency 4 on the overhead. Expose 2 rows of 6 squares each, using one piece of paper to mask the lower 8 rows and another piece of paper to mask the 4 columns on the right.

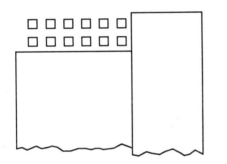

Ask, "How many rows? (2) How many squares in each row? (6) How many squares in all? (12)" Have students tell how they determined the total. (Think double 6, or 6 + 6 = 12.) Repeat the activity, exposing different numbers of squares in each of 2 rows.

Next, expose 4 rows with 6 squares in each row. Ask, "How many rows? How many squares in each row?" Place a pen or pencil between the second and third rows. Ask, "How many rows are above the pen? (2) How many rows are below? (2) How many squares are above the pen? (12) How many squares are below? (12) How many squares are there in all? (12 + 12 or 24)"

Repeat the activity, showing 4 rows of 5 squares each, 4 rows of 3 squares, 4 rows of 7 squares, and 4 rows of 10 squares.

EXTENDING THE LESSON
Without letting students see what you are doing, use masks on the transparency to prepare a display of 4 rows with 6 squares in each row.

Cover the display with another piece of paper. For this activity, remove the covering paper for one second or less, then return it. Tell the students that there were 4 rows. Ask, "How many squares were there in all? (24)"

Not all students will have seen 6 squares in each row. Allow them to explain their responses. If a student saw 5 in each row, he or she may say something to the effect that 2 rows of 5 is 10, and 10 + 10 is 20. If so, this should be considered a "good" response. Accept all answers that have adequate explanations. Then show the 24 squares.

Repeat, showing 4 rows of 7, 4 rows of 3, 4 rows of 8, and 4 rows of 10.

ORAL FOLLOW-UP
1. Ask students to calculate the following in their heads:

Double 12 (24)	Double 10 (20)
Double 14 (28)	Double 8 (16)
Double 15 (30)	Double 6 (12)
Double 16 (32)	Double 18 (36)

For the problems that students find difficult, suggest that they first double just the tens digit, then double the ones digit, and add them together. That is, for double 16 they would think, "Double 10 = 20; double 6 = 12; 20 and 12 = 32."

2. Ask students to double the following numbers, then double the result.

Double 4. Now double again. (16)
Double 3. Now double again. (12)
Double 5. Now double again. (20)
Double 8. Now double again. (32)
Double 7. Now double again. (28)
Double 2. Now double again. (8)
Double 9. Now double again. (36)
Double 10. Now double again. (40)
Double 6. Now double again. (24)

3. Try these triple doubles:

Double 2. Now double that. Now double again. (16)

Double 3. Now double that. Now double again. (24)

Double 4. Now double that. Now double again. (32)

Double 5. Now double that. Now double again. (40)

Double 6. Now double that. Now double again. (48)

Lesson 5   Using a Double

ABOUT THE LESSON
Once students can easily recall the sum of any double from 1 to 9, they can use those basic facts to help them learn other addition facts. This lesson shows students how they can use their skill in doubling to mentally work out addition combinations with numbers that are close to a double (such as 3 + 4, or 7 + 9).

YOU WILL NEED . . .
• Transparency 5, "Doubles Plus 1 or 2"
• Power Builder 2, page 90

TEACHING THE LESSON
Place Transparency 5 on the overhead. Cover all but the picture at the top. On the double-frame dot picture, point out that there are 4 dots above and 5 dots below, but that if we look at it another way, this picture shows a double *and some more*. Ask students to find the double. (4 + 4) Circle the double-four pattern with an overhead pen. Then ask, "How many more than double 4 is there? (1 more)" Explain that we can quickly figure the total number of dots by looking for a double (4 + 4), then adding 1 more; that is, 4 + 4 = 8, and 1 more makes 9.

Continue in this way with the other dot pictures. Have the students first identify the double in each picture, then state the total number of dots. For the last four pictures, students will have to add 2 to the doubled number.

Next, have students double given numbers and add 1 or 2, as follows:

Double 4 and add 1.	Double 8 and add 2.
Double 6 and add 1.	Double 6 and add 2.
Double 7 and add 1.	Double 3 and add 1.
Double 3 and add 2.	Double 4 and add 2.
Double 5 and add 2.	Double 7 and add 2.

Write the addition fact 4 + 5 on the board or overhead. Ask students how they might use a double to help them think out the answer. (Think double 4 [or 4 + 4] = 8, and 1 more makes 9.) If they have trouble seeing this, refer back to the dot-picture at the top of Transparency 5 for a visual model of 4 + 5.

Present the following addition exercises, telling students to think of a double that will help them find the answer. Have them state (or write) the

double they would use in each case. If they find this difficult, suggest that they visualize each fact as a dot picture.

3 + 4 (7)	6 + 7 (13)
5 + 6 (11)	4 + 5 (9)
8 + 9 (17)	7 + 6 (13)
6 + 5 (11)	4 + 3 (7)
5 + 4 (9)	9 + 8 (17)

EXTENDING THE LESSON
1. Ask students to add 1 or 2 to larger doubles, as follows:

Double 12 and add 1 (25)
Double 10 and add 2 (22)
Double 14 and add 1 (29)
Double 11 and add 2 (24)
Double 24 and add 1 (49)
Double 32 and add 2 (66)

Repeat with other two-digit numbers, keeping both digits 5 or less.

2. Ask students to tell how they could use doubling to find sums like the following:

12 + 13 (double 12, add 1)
10 + 12 (double 10, add 2)
11 + 12 (double 11, add 1)
24 + 25 (double 24, add 1)
32 + 34 (double 32, add 2)

Continue with other combinations in which the addends are 1 or 2 apart.

ORAL FOLLOW-UP
Present students with "doubles-plus-2" combinations like those listed below. Have them say or write the double they would use to help them find the answer.

4 + 6 (double 4 plus 2 = 10)
5 + 7 (double 5 plus 2 = 12)
3 + 5 (double 3 plus 2 = 8)
7 + 9 (double 7 plus 2 = 16)
6 + 8 (double 6 plus 2 = 14)
7 + 5 (double 5 plus 2 = 12)
5 + 3 (double 3 plus 2 = 8)
6 + 4 (double 4 plus 2 = 10)
9 + 7 (double 7 plus 2 = 16)

INDIVIDUAL PRACTICE
Distribute copies of Power Builder 2 for more practice in using doubles.

Lesson 6   Adding to Make Ten

ABOUT THE LESSON

Ten serves as the basis of our number system and plays a key role in many of the mental math strategies students will be learning. Consequently, students need to be very familiar with combinations that add to make ten (6 + 4, 3 + 7, and so on). In *Mental Math in the Middle Grades,* students will come to recognize pairs of numbers that "make ten" as *compatible numbers*—so-called because together they make a tidy sum that is easy to work with mentally.

Once students have mastered as basic number facts these addition combinations that make ten, they will find them useful in learning other facts, as well. The combinations will also be used in later lessons for work with multidigit numbers.

YOU WILL NEED . . .

• Counters
• Transparency 6, "Ten-Frame"

TEACHING THE LESSON

Place Transparency 6 on the overhead and put 7 counters on the empty ten-frame. Fill the first row with 5 counters and place 2 counters in the second row. Discuss the frame with students, pointing out that each row of the frame contains 5 boxes. We can readily tell the number of objects in the ten-frame by counting forward or backward from 5, or backward from 10. For example, in the case just set up, we recognize at a glance that one full row equals 5, then we count up the 2 in the next row *(five . . . SIX, SEVEN)* to determine how many boxes are filled.

Point out further that when 7 boxes have counters in them, 3 are empty—for a total of 7 + 3, or 10. There will always be 10 boxes; when a certain number are filled, another certain number will be empty.

Now place 8 counters in the ten-frame and display it briefly (one second or less). Have students write both the number of counters and the number of empty boxes they saw. Ask if those numbers add to make ten. Repeat this activity with different numbers of counters. Remind students to be sure that the two numbers make ten in each case.

EXTENDING THE LESSON

Once students are comfortable with the pairs that make ten, you can extend the lesson by giving them pairs that don't make ten, or that make ten plus some more. Initially, this helps them determine whether or not "making tens" is a useful strategy in a particular case. It also offers a preview of the strategy introduced in lesson 9, adding larger numbers by first making ten.

Out of the students' view, place 6 counters in the ten-frame and 3 counters beside it. Display this arrangement briefly (one second or less). Ask students to guess if the loose counters will fill up the ten-frame. Then ask, "Are there more than 10 counters altogether, or less than 10? How many more or less?" Repeat the activity, using the following numbers of counters:

7 in the ten-frame, 4 outside
5 in the ten-frame, 5 outside
8 in the ten-frame, 1 outside
6 in the ten-frame, 6 outside
9 in the ten-frame, 3 outside

Continue with other combinations.

ORAL FOLLOW-UP

1. Tell students to picture an empty ten-frame in their minds. Explain that you are going to put imaginary counters into their imaginary ten-frames. As you state the number of counters you have put in the ten-frame, the students are to write the number of empty boxes.

YOU SAY	STUDENTS WRITE	YOU SAY	STUDENTS WRITE
8	2	7	3
3	7	0	10
6	4	4	6
5	5	9	1

2. Have individuals stand before the group, raise both hands, and briefly hold up some fingers. Challenge the group to tell how many fingers were held up and how many were down.

3. Present oral problems that involve adding to make ten. For example:

• Juan liked to wear rings. He had rings on all but 3 of his fingers. How many of his fingers did not have rings? (7 fingers)

• At the school fair, Gina bought a purple crayon for 4¢. She paid with a dime. How much change did she receive? (6¢)

• When ten-pin bowling, Larry knocked over 8 pins. How many were left standing? (2 pins)

• To get his name on the RIP (Reading is Praiseworthy) list, Kevin has to read 10 books. He has already read 5. How many more does he need to read? (5 books)

• Darla set up 10 cans on the fence and tossed snowballs at them. First she knocked over 3 cans, then she knocked over 4 more. How many cans were left on the fence? (3 cans)

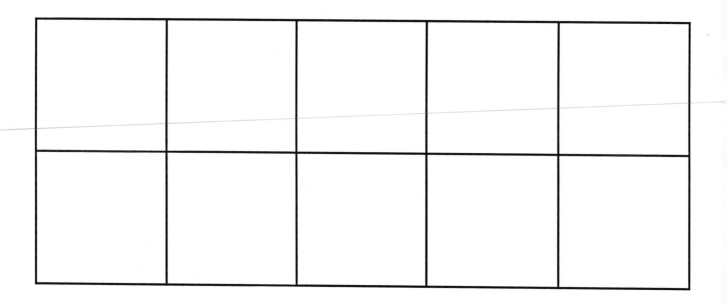

Lesson 7   Adding with Tens

ABOUT THE LESSON
The mental math skill presented in this lesson is adding 10 or a multiple of 10 to a single number. This is an important basic skill in numeration and place value; it also forms the basis for mentally adding 8 and 9 to a number.

Rather than counting on to determine the answer, students are encouraged to recognize the pattern and simply combine the ones and ten(s). That is, they should see that 40 + 3 makes 43, because 40 is 4 tens, and 4 tens and 3 ones is written 43.

For some of the activities in this lesson, you are told to show a visual model to the students very briefly—for a second a less. This timing is important. If you allow students more than a short time to view the model, they may rely on counting to determine the answer.

YOU WILL NEED . . .
• Transparency 7, "Adding with Ten(s)"

TEACHING THE LESSON
Place Transparency 7 on the overhead, covering all but the ten-frame at the top. Draw 6 dots next to the ten-frame and ask how many dots there are in all. (16) Write that answer beside the picture. Point out that we can think of this as 1 ten (the ten-frame) and 6 ones (the loose dots), and 1 ten and 6 ones is the same as 16. Repeat the activity, drawing different numbers of dots next to the ten-frame.

Next, out of the students' view, draw 7 dots next to the ten-frame. Cover both the frame and the dots with a piece of paper. Explain that you are going to show them the ten-frame and some loose dots for about one second. They are to tell you the total number of dots they see. After briefly exposing the picture, ask for responses. Responding students must tell you how many tens and how many ones they saw. Reinforce the concept that 1 ten and 7 ones is the same as 17.

Treat any answer as "good" if the student's response corresponds to what he or she reported seeing, even though the answer is not right for the model shown. For instance, if the student reported seeing 8 extra dots and responded 18, that is a "good" answer.

Repeat the activity, drawing 4 extra dots this time.

Next, expose the hundreds square at the bottom of the transparency. (Be sure that students recognize it as a hundreds square.) Shade in the first 4 full columns going up and down, then shade in 6 extra squares in the next column, starting from the bottom. Ask how many squares are shaded in all. Emphasize the concept that 4 tens and 6 ones is the same as 46. Repeat, shading in other numbers of full columns and extra squares.

Next announce that you are going to briefly show the hundreds square with a certain number of squares already shaded in. Students are to look carefully to determine the number. Out of their view, shade in 28 squares (2 full columns plus 8 squares in the next column, starting from the bottom). Expose this picture for one second or less and ask how many squares were shaded in all. Responding students must tell how many tens and how many ones they saw. If the answer reflects what they saw (even though what they saw was inaccurate), it is considered a "good" answer. Allow several students to respond.

Repeat the activity, each time briefly exposing the hundreds square with varying numbers of squares shaded in.

EXTENDING THE LESSON
State the following combinations and have students write the total for each.

   1 ten and 6 ones (16)
   1 ten and 5 ones (15)
   7 ones and 1 ten (17)
   3 ones and 1 ten (13)
   9 dimes and 1 penny (91¢)
   2 tens and 5 ones (25)
   8 dimes and 4 pennies (84¢)
   7 tens and 9 ones (79)
   5 tens and 2 ones (52)
   7 ones and 3 tens (37)
   4 pennies and 7 dimes (74¢)
   1 one and 6 tens (61)

Continue with other combinations if students seem to need more practice.

ORAL FOLLOW-UP
1. Present the following exercises, allowing students only 3 seconds to respond before you state the next one.

4 + 10 (14)	5 + 10 (15)	10 + 7 (17)
10 + 9 (19)	6 + 10 (16)	10 + 8 (18)
10 + 2 (12)	10 + 1 (11)	3 + 10 (13)

2. Repeat the above activity with combinations that involve adding single-digit numbers to multiples of ten, as follows:

50 + 6 (56)	70 + 3 (73)	90 + 7 (97)
4 + 60 (64)	9 + 20 (29)	5 + 80 (85)
30 + 1 (31)	70 + 8 (78)	10 + 6 (16)

Lesson 8   Adding 8 and 9

ABOUT THE LESSON
This lesson builds on the preceding two. Once students can quickly determine what number to add to another to make ten (lesson 6), that skill will help them with other basic addition facts, especially facts involving 8 and 9. For instance, to add 8 and 5, students can mentally "make ten" by adding 8 and 2, then add the remaining 3 to get 13.

To be successful with this lesson, students should be proficient with the tens facts, especially 8 + 2 and 9 + 1. They should also be able to quickly add 10 to any one-digit number (10 + 3, 10 + 6, 10 + 5, and so on), as discussed in lesson 7.

YOU WILL NEED . . .
• Transparency 8, "Adding 8 and 9"
• Counters
• Power Builder 3, page 91

TEACHING THE LESSON
Place Transparency 8 on the overhead, exposing only the top ten-frame. Ask how many counters are in the frame. (9) Place 5 loose counters just below this ten-frame, pointing out that the addition combination now shown is 9 + 5. Move 1 of the 5 loose counters into the empty box of the ten-frame. Ask, "What addition combination is shown now? (10 + 4) What is the total? (14)"

Repeat, using a different number of loose counters.

Next, cover the top of Transparency 8 and expose the ten-frame at the bottom, which contains 8 counters. Repeat the procedures above, having students identify the various addition combinations you show.

EXTENDING THE LESSON
Present addition combinations involving 8 and 9, asking students to write the tens fact that will help them find the answer to the combination. For instance, if you give 9 + 5, the students should say 10 + 4. If you give 8 + 6, the students should say 10 + 4.

Ask students to say or write the tens facts they would use to find the total for the following combinations:

9 + 6	9 + 7	9 + 4
5 + 9	3 + 9	8 + 9
2 + 9	8 + 4	8 + 5
8 + 7	8 + 3	6 + 8

ORAL FOLLOW-UP
1. Ask the students to find the total for each of the following addition combinations. Remind them to think first of a tens fact to help them.

3 + 9 (12)	8 + 5 (13)
9 + 4 (13)	7 + 9 (16)
8 + 4 (12)	6 + 8 (14)
5 + 9 (14)	9 + 3 (12)
6 + 9 (15)	8 + 6 (14)

2. Present the following story problems. Suggest that students think of "making ten" to help them find each answer.

• Tom needed a dime to put in a vending machine. He reached in one pocket and pulled out 8 cents. He reached in his shoe and found 4 more cents. He traded in 10 of the pennies for a dime. How many pennies did he have left? (2 pennies) How much money did he have in all? (12 cents)

• Kara was stacking boxes in rows of 10. She had 9 boxes in one pile and 6 boxes in another one. She made one row and had some boxes left over. How many boxes were left over? (5 boxes) How many boxes did she have in all? (15 boxes)

• Luisa and Sean played a game in which each of them held up a certain number of fingers. During one round of the game, Sean held up 8 fingers and Luisa held up 6 fingers. How many fingers did they hold up together? (14 fingers)

• In one section of the kennel, there are 2 rows of cages with 5 cages in each row. Nine of the cages contain dogs. Four more dogs are brought into the kennel and need cages. How many dogs are there in all? (13 dogs)

Make up similar story problems that can be solved by first "making ten."

INDIVIDUAL PRACTICE
Distribute copies of Power Builder 3 for more practice in making ten and adding with ten.

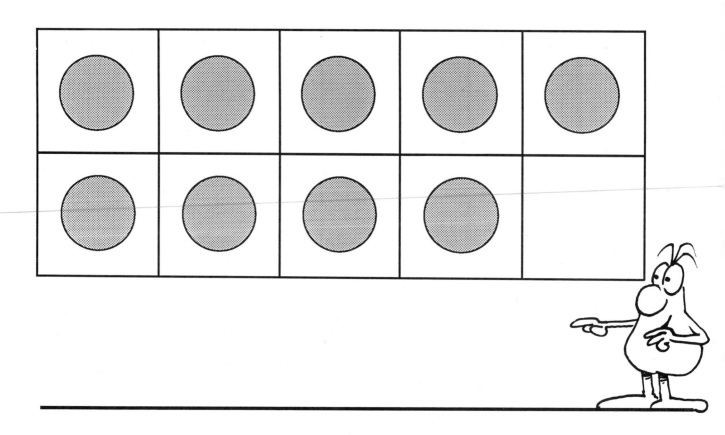

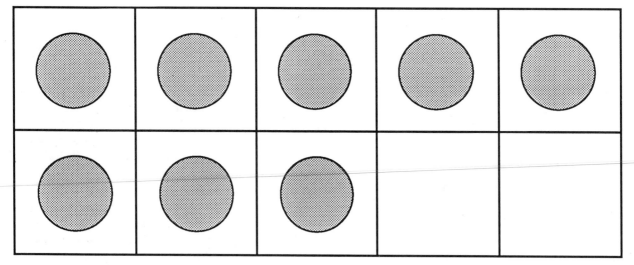

Lesson 9   Adding Larger Numbers by "Making Tens"

ABOUT THE LESSON

This lesson extends the "making tens" principle to work with larger numbers. That is, once the students know how to find the answer to 9 + 4 by thinking "9 plus 1 is 10, plus 3 is 13," they should be able to find the answer to 19 + 4 in much the same way.

YOU WILL NEED . . .
- Transparency 9, "Make Tens to Add"
- Power Builders 4 and 5, pages 92–93

TEACHING THE LESSON

Write the addition combination 9 + 6 on the board. Ask the students to make ten and determine the answer. (15) Then write the combination 19 + 6 on the board.

Place Transparency 9 on the overhead, exposing only the top section. Point out the two ten-frames that contain a total of 19 dots. Explain that you are going to show the combination 19 + 6, and draw 6 loose dots below the frame containing 9. Ask students how many dots are needed to fill the second frame. (1) Erase 1 loose dot and draw it in the empty box. Ask, "How many dots are there in all? (25, or 2 full frames and 5 more)" Explain that we have just used "making tens" to find the answer to the combination on the board, 19 + 6.

Now write the combination 28 + 5 and expose the bottom section of the transparency. Point out the three ten-frames containing 28 dots. To show 28 + 5, draw 5 loose dots below the frame containing 8. Ask how many dots are needed to fill that frame (2), then erase 2 loose dots and draw them in the empty boxes. Ask, "How many dots are there altogether? (33)"

For additional practice, use the same transparency but draw dots to represent different combinations, such as 19 + 8, 19 + 5, 19 + 3, 28 + 4, 28 + 6, and 28 + 7.

EXTENDING THE LESSON

Present pairs of related addition combinations like the ones shown below. Suggest that students use the answer to the first one to help them find the answer to the second.

8 + 5 (13),	28 + 5 (33)
9 + 6 (15),	49 + 6 (55)
3 + 8 (11),	53 + 8 (61)

7 + 9 (16),	87 + 9 (96)
8 + 4 (12),	28 + 4 (32)
9 + 3 (12),	69 + 3 (72)
5 + 9 (14),	15 + 9 (24)
7 + 8 (15),	77 + 8 (85)
7 + 6 (13),	57 + 6 (63)
4 + 7 (11),	84 + 7 (91)

ORAL FOLLOW-UP

Present the following story problems. Encourage students to "make ten" to help them find the answers.

- Marty had 58¢. He received another 8¢ from his sister for helping her with her homework. (He didn't help her all that much!) How much money does Marty have now? (66¢)

- Celeste was setting out tomato plants. Her mother told her to plant them in rows of 10. After Celeste had planted 29 tomatoes, she stopped to rest and have a snack, leaving 6 plants yet to be set out. Altogether, how many tomato plants will Celeste set out? (35 plants)

- When Sara was 6, her father was 38. Now Sara is 12. How old is her father? (44)

- At the start of the school year, Mario was in a class of 19 students. Then the 5 Gilbert girls—they were quintuplets—came to town. All of them joined Mario's class. How many students are in that class now? (24 students)

- Right now it is 10:37. What time will it be in 8 minutes? (10:45)

- Kasandra measured 58 inches tall when she was in fourth grade. Over the summer she grew 5 inches. How tall was she when she started fifth grade? (63 inches)

- The elevator broke down as Kent was riding to his father's office. He had to get out on the 27th floor and walk up the remaining 6 floors to the office. On what floor does Kent's father work? (33rd floor)

- Near the end of the bicycle race, Heather noticed she had already ridden 48 kilometers. If she had exactly 4 kilometers yet to go, how long was the race? (52 kilometers)

INDIVIDUAL PRACTICE

Distribute copies of Power Builders 4 and 5 for timed mental practice in the basic addition facts.

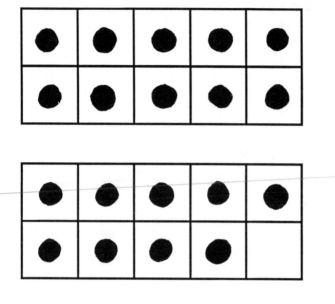

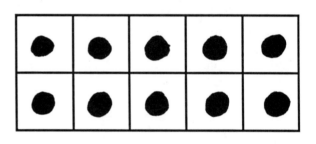

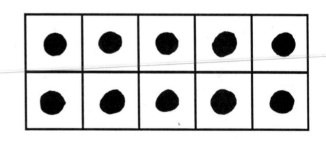

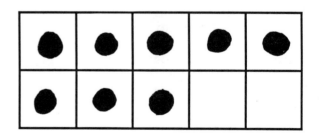

Unit One Progress Test

The fifteen-item test below, intended for timed oral presentation, is designed to measure students' mental computation skills in the concepts presented in Unit One.

Have the students write their names at the top of a sheet of lined paper and number from 1 to 15. Instruct them to write the answer to each problem after the proper number. Emphasize that they will have only 5 seconds to compute the answer in their heads and write it before you go on to the next problem.

Read the problem number, then the problem. Repeat it, wait 5 to 7 seconds, then read the next question.

UNIT ONE TEST		ANSWERS	
1.	2 plus 9	1.	11
2.	7 plus 3	2.	10
3.	46 and 3 more	3.	49
4.	6 plus 6	4.	12
5.	double 8	5.	16
6.	double 14	6.	28
7.	7 plus 8	7.	15
8.	6 plus 5	8.	11
9.	What do you add to 7 to make 10?	9.	3
10.	2 plus what makes 10?	10.	8
11.	4 plus 10	11.	14
12.	10 plus 7	12.	17
13.	9 plus 6	13.	15
14.	5 plus 8	14.	13
15.	29 plus 5	15.	34

Thinking Strategies for Subtraction

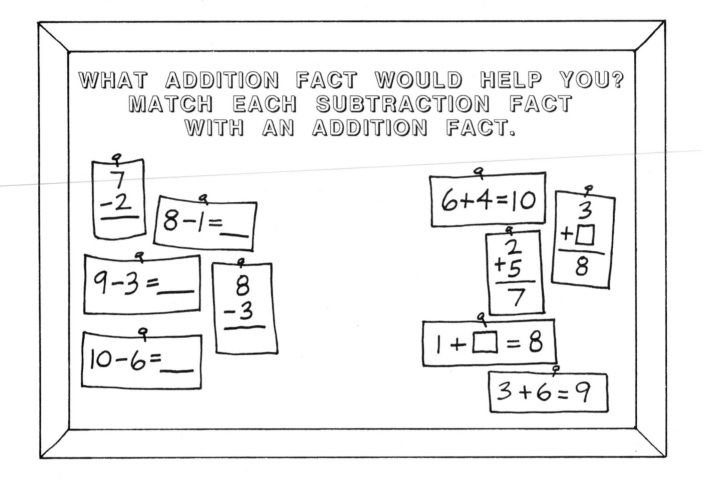

WHAT ADDITION FACT WOULD HELP YOU?
MATCH EACH SUBTRACTION FACT
WITH AN ADDITION FACT.

$$\begin{array}{r}7\\-2\\\hline\end{array}$$

$8-1=\underline{\quad}$

$9-3=\underline{\quad}$

$$\begin{array}{r}8\\-3\\\hline\end{array}$$

$10-6=\underline{\quad}$

$6+4=10$

$$\begin{array}{r}2\\+5\\\hline 7\end{array}$$

$$\begin{array}{r}3\\+\square\\\hline 8\end{array}$$

$1+\square=8$

$3+6=9$

$14-8=\underline{\quad}$ $8+6=14$

UNIT TWO OVERVIEW

The thinking strategies that students can use as they learn the basic subtraction facts include *counting back, counting up,* and *thinking addition.* Counting back is a useful strategy for subtracting 1, 2, or 3 from a number (4 – 1, 9 – 3, 8 – 2, and so on). Counting up works well when the numbers are just 1, 2, or 3 apart (as in 9 – 7, 12 – 9, 10 – 9). Thinking addition to determine the answer to a subtraction combination is the most useful strategy of all. However, it requires a sophistication that not all students will initially possess. *Counting back* and *counting up* give the students simple strategies to use for subtraction while they are working on the more difficult *thinking addition* strategy.

The beauty of thinking addition is this: If students can be taught to use the addition facts they *know* to find the answers to subtraction combinations they *don't know,* in essence they have to learn only one set of basic facts. This leaves more time for developing the mental skills involved in applying the basic facts in problem-solving situations. You will find it easier to develop the thinking addition strategy if you avoid drilling for mastery of the subtraction combinations until the students have mastered related addition facts.

Otherwise, drill with subtraction facts should proceed much the same way as drill with addition facts. The five Power Builder pages for this unit provide structured, timed practice of appropriate facts. The first three are designed for use after specific lessons; the next two are a collection of basic subtraction facts and are to be used after you have completed the entire unit. As with the Power Builders in Unit One, remember to allow 50 seconds for completion of the first row, 40 seconds for the second, 30 for the third, and 20 for the fourth. Later, as students' skills improve, you can decrease the times allowed.

BULLETIN BOARD FOR UNIT TWO

The major goal of this unit is to develop in students the ability to think addition when given a subtraction combination. The suggested bulletin board illustrated opposite offers students practice in selecting addition facts they know that can help them find the answers to subtraction combinations.

You will need an assortment of cards containing addition facts, some with the same "part" and "total" as one of the subtraction combinations. That is, for the subtraction card 8 – 3 = 5, you would need a card for the addition fact 3 + 5 = 8. Students are to tack the related addition card next to the appropriate subtraction combination and solve. In preparing the cards, keep the addition fact in the same format as the related subtraction combination (horizontal or vertical). Include some addition facts with missing parts, such as 4 + __ = 11.

Lesson 10   Counting Back

ABOUT THE LESSON
Counting back can be used to subtract 1, 2, or 3 from a number. To be comfortable with this strategy, students need to be able to count backwards from any given number. Provide practice in this skill as necessary.

YOU WILL NEED . . .
- Transparency 10, "Counting Back"
- Counters
- Power Builder 6, page 94

TEACHING THE LESSON
Place 6 counters in one of your hands, and tell the students how many you are holding. Drop 1 counter and ask, "How many counters are still in my hand?" Tell them to start with 6 and count back 1 *(6 . . . 5)*. Repeat, holding 6 counters but dropping 2 counters (one at a time). Have the students count back from 6 as the counters fall from your hand, first saying "six" to themselves quietly, then the count-back numbers more loudly *(six . . . FIVE, FOUR)*.

Continue with this activity, variously hiding 7, 8, and 9 counters in your hand and dropping 1, 2, or 3 counters.

Place Transparency 10 on the overhead and cover all but the picture at the top. Write an 8 in the box beside the pouch and tell this story:

Katy had 8 beads in a little leather pouch. But the pouch had a split in the seam, and 2 of her beads fell out. How many beads are still in the pouch?

Have the students write or state the number of beads left in the pouch. Encourage them to count back from 8 to find the answer.

Go on the the second picture. Write 6 in the box beside the chest and tell this story:

Elena had 6 robots in a wooden chest. She took out 3 to play with. How many robots are left in the chest? (Have students count back to determine the answer.)

For the last picture, write 9 in the box behind the wagon and tell this story:

Adam was giving 9 bears a ride in his wagon. When it hit a bump, 1 bear fell out. How many bears are still riding in the wagon? (Have students count back to determine the answer.)

Repeat the activity with different one-digit numbers and different stories.

EXTENDING THE LESSON
1. Repeat the lesson activities, but in each case have students write the subtraction sentence represented by the picture and story.
2. Repeat the lesson activities, writing two-digit numbers in the boxes.

ORAL FOLLOW-UP
1. Present situations that call for subtracting 1, 2, or 3 from a number that is 10 or less. Use a variety of wordings, similar to the following:

What is 2 less than 8? (6)

What is 9 minus 3? (6)

If you count back 1 from 7, at what number are you? (6)

What is 10 take away 2? (8)

If you subtract 2 from 6, how much is that? (4)

2. Present story problems that involve counting back 1, 2, or 3 to find the answer. For example:
- Mr. Weaver, the school principal, had a hole in his pocket. When he left home, he had 8 nickels. On his way to the school, 3 nickels fell out. How many nickels did Mr. Weaver have in his pocket when he got to school? (5 nickels)
- Jamie tried to hide 7 marbles in her hand. Since her hand was small and the marbles were big, she couldn't hold them all and 2 fell out. How many marbles stayed in her hand? (5 marbles)
- Usually there are 9 players on Mark's team. Today 2 of the players are sick and did not come to practice. How many players are at practice? (7 players)
- Perched on a limb of the big oak tree were 10 swallows. Two flew away to look for swallow food to swallow. How many swallows are left perched on the limb? (8 swallows)

Present problems with similar wordings for situations that involve subtracting 1, 2, or 3.

INDIVIDUAL PRACTICE
Distribute copies of Power Builder 6 for more practice in counting back 1, 2, or 3.

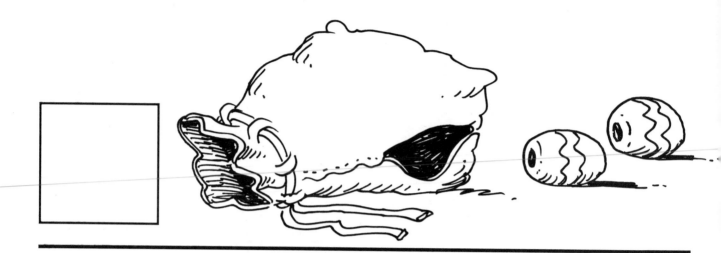

Lesson 11   Counting Up

ABOUT THE LESSON

While *counting back* helps students subtract 1, 2, or 3, it is not an efficient procedure to use for subtracting larger numbers. A different strategy can help if the two numbers being compared are of nearly equal size: *counting up*. That is, when the difference between two numbers is 3 or less, we can easily determine that difference by counting up from the smaller number to the larger. To calculate 9 – 7, we would say the 7 quietly, then count up to 9 *(seven . . . EIGHT, NINE)*. Since we counted 2 more than 7 to reach 9, 9 – 7 = 2. Note that students may need to use fingers to keep track as they count.

YOU WILL NEED . . .

- Counters
- Transparency 11, "Counting Up to Subtract"
- Power Builder 7, page 95

TEACHING THE LESSON

Place 9 counters in view of the students. Cover the counters with a sheet of paper; then slide 7 counters out from under the sheet. Explain, "I have removed 7 counters. How many counters are still under the paper?" Encourage students to start from 7 and count up, "seven [softly] . . . EIGHT, NINE." Emphasize using fingers to keep track of the count. (You might encourage more capable students to add on, instead.)

Repeat, starting with 10 counters under the sheet and sliding out 7. Continue with other numbers, always leaving a remainder of 1, 2, or 3.

Place Transparency 11 on the overhead. Point out the picture of the doghouse at the top. Write a 9 in the box next to the house. Explain:

There were 9 puppies in the doghouse, but these 7 puppies came outside to play. How many puppies are still in the doghouse? (Encourage counting up from 7.)

Write an 8 in the box beside the picture of the van. Explain:

Eight people were riding in the van and these 6 got out to go to the ballpark. How many people are left in the van? (Encourage counting up from 6.)

Point out the paper bag and write a 10 in the box beside it. Explain:

Taylor had 10 peanuts in a bag that he put outside for the squirrels. One squirrel took 7 of the peanuts. How many peanuts are left in the bag? (Encourage counting up from 7.)

Repeat the activity, using different numbers for each picture. With the doghouse, you can write 10 and 8 in the box. With the van, use 9, 6, and 7. With the peanuts, use 8 and 9. Encourage students to count up from the smaller number.

Point to the bottom section of the transparency. Write 12 in the box, telling students that there were 12 coins in the change jar. Then write a 9 in the hand, explaining that Gene took 9 coins out of the jar. Ask, "How many coins are left inside?" Repeat this activity with other pairs of numbers that are 1, 2, or 3 apart.

EXTENDING THE LESSON

1. For each of the situations presented on the lesson transparency, have the students write the subtraction sentence represented.

2. Repeat the activity with the coins in the jar (bottom of the transparency), using pairs of larger numbers that differ by 1, 2, or 3; for example, 24 and 22; 45 and 44; 65 and 62; 76 and 74; 39 and 36; and so forth.

ORAL FOLLOW-UP

1. Present subtraction situations involving differences of just 1, 2, or 3. Use a variety of wordings similar to the following:

How many more than 7 is 9? (2)
How many fewer than 10 is 8? (2)
How many do you add to 9 to make 12? (3)
When you take 7 away from 8, how many are left? (1)
What is the difference between 9 and 11? (2)
What is 10 – 7? 9 – 6? 11 – 8? 10 – 9?

2. Present story problems involving differences of 1, 2, or 3. For example:

- Vic needs 10 cents to buy a pencil but has only 8 cents. How much more does he need? (2 cents)

- Stephanie had 6 tapes in her collection. Jenny had 9 in hers. How many fewer tapes did Stephanie have than Jenny? (3 tapes)

- To win a bike, Joanna had to sell 12 more magazine subscriptions. She worked really hard and sold 10 to her relatives. How many more subscriptions did she need to sell? (2 subscriptions)

- Marty has 7 T-shirts, some blue and some red. If 5 are red, how many are blue? (2 T-shirts)

- Mike is 5 and his younger brother is only 3. How much older is Mike? (2 years)

INDIVIDUAL PRACTICE

Distribute copies of Power Builder 7 for more practice in counting up to subtract.

Lesson 12   Partitioning

OVERVIEW, LESSONS 12–15

Counting back (lesson 10) is an effective way to mentally subtract the numbers 1, 2, and 3; and counting up (lesson 11) is useful for finding differences of 3 or less. However, a generally much more efficient way to subtract is to recall a related addition combination. For the subtraction combination $13 - 7$, we can readily determine the answer if we think, "I know that $7 + 6 = 13$, so $13 - 7$ must be 6." Young students must acquire several skills before they can subtract by recalling a known addition combination. The purpose of the next three lessons is to develop these foundation skills before the actual *thinking addition* strategy is presented in lesson 15.

ABOUT THE LESSON

Partitioning is one of the basic skills underlying the ability to subtract by thinking addition. In partitioning, we take a total—such as 13—and break it into two parts—such as 6 and 7, or 9 and 4, or 8 and 5. Note that we will always use the words *part, part,* and *total* when referring to addition facts rather than the terms *addend* and *sum*.

In this lesson, the students will practice identifying all the addition combinations for a particular total. For instance, students should come to recognize that $1 + 5$, $2 + 4$, and $3 + 3$ are all names for 6. Six is the *total*, and 1 and 5 (or 2 and 4, or 3 and 3) are *parts* that add to make 6.

YOU WILL NEED . . .

• Counters
• Transparency 12, "Part + Part = Total"

TEACHING THE LESSON

Place Transparency 12 on the overhead. Put 6 counters in the right side of the empty frame. Write a 6 in the box above the frame. Tell the students that this number represents the *total* number of counters being used. Slide 2 counters from the right to the left side of the frame.

Explain that this display shows us that the total is 6, and two parts that make 6 are 2 and 4. Ask students to name some other parts that add together to make 6. (1 and 5, 3 and 3) As the students say each pair of parts, move the counters in the frame to represent them. Below the frame, list all the different pairs of parts that total 6.

Repeat the activity, starting with 7 counters in the right side of the frame. Remember to write a 7 in the box above the frame. Again, list all the pairs of parts that total 7. Continue with 8, 9, and 10 counters.

EXTENDING THE LESSON

Give students a total, such as 8. Have them write all the pairs of parts that total 8. (1 and 7; 2 and 6; 3 and 5; 4 and 4; 0 and 8) Check to see if the students have missed any. Repeat, giving totals of 9, 10, 11, 12, and 13.

ORAL FOLLOW-UP

1. Present a variety of partitioning situations, as follows:

I'm thinking of two parts that total 7. One of them is a 2. What is the other part? (5)

Write two parts that total 8. One of them must be a 3. (3, 5)

The total is 10 and one of the parts is 7. What is the other part? (3)

Repeat similar questions using other numbers.

2. Play a guessing game based on partitioning. Group students into teams of 5 or 6 each and keep track of team scores. Explain:

I'm thinking of two parts that total 8. You guess what they are. If you guess correctly, your team receives 2 points. If you guess a different pair that total 8, your team receives 1 point.

Continue with other totals. You might write each pair you are thinking of on a concealed pad, then reveal it when students guess correctly.

Total
Parts

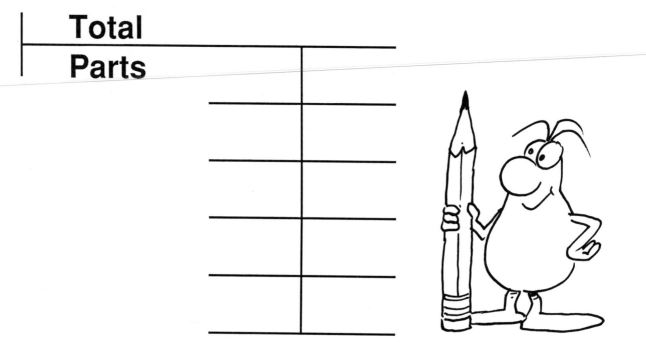

Lesson 13   Missing Parts

ABOUT THE LESSON
Sometimes we state an addition fact with a missing part; for example, $8 + \_\_ = 13$. Finding the missing part in a fact stated this way is an important mental skill for students to develop as you lay the groundwork for thinking addition in subtraction. Once students can "think addition" and determine the missing part when looking at a subtraction exercise, they will be able to subtract numbers faster and more accurately.

In this lesson, students will be asked to find the missing parts in addition facts for sums from 9 to 18. Your emphasis should be on the sums 9, 10, and 11 since these numbers involve the most basic fact combinations.

YOU WILL NEED . . .
Transparency 13, "Missing Parts"

TEACHING THE LESSON
Place Transparency 13 on the overhead and cover the bottom picture. Focus attention on the row of 10 pennies. Count them with the students; then cover up 4 of the coins. Explain:

Juan had 10 cents, then he spent some on a jaw breaker, and now he has 6 cents left. What is the missing part here? 6 plus what makes 10? How much did Juan spend?

Using the names of your students, present other stories about spending, losing, or sharing some of the 10 cents. Cover up differing numbers of coins each time. Help students see each problem in terms of finding the missing part.

Next uncover the bottom picture to show the birdhouse with the 12 birds flying around outside it. Count them with the students; then cover up 8 of the birds. Explain:

A big yellow cat scared away some birds so that now only 4 are left. How many birds were scared away?

Help them see the problem as an addition fact with a missing part: $4 + \_\_ = 12$. (8)

Present other stories about the birds, covering up a different number of them each time. You might use situations like these: How many flew south for the winter? How many went for a splash in the fountain? How many are asleep in the birdhouse? How many flew off to find a new place to live?

EXTENDING THE LESSON
Place 5 counters in one hand and 6 in the other. Tell the students that you have 11 counters altogether. Show them the 6 counters and ask, "How many counters are in my other hand?"

Repeat the activity, placing 4 counters in one hand and 7 in the other. Continue with other combinations that total 11, then repeat the activity using totals of 10, 12, and 13 counters.

ORAL FOLLOW-UP
Ask "missing part" questions, using wording similar to that in the examples below:

Six plus what number makes 10? (4)

What do we need to add to 8 to make 12? (4)

If one part is 7 and the total is 13, what is the other part? (6)

Add on to 5 to make 14. What did you add? (9)

How much greater than 9 is 12? (3)

How much less than 11 is 7? (4)

Lesson 14   Corner Cover-Up

ABOUT THE LESSON
This lesson presents a visual model to help students grasp the interrelation of the three elements in a basic fact—part, part, and total. The point is to help them think of subtraction as simply another form of addition, which can make it easier for them to learn the subtraction facts. In the visual model, the two parts and the total are placed at the corners of a triangle. Whenever any one of those three numbers is covered, students should be able to identify its value just by seeing the other numbers.

YOU WILL NEED . . .
• Transparency 14, "Corner Cover-Up"

TEACHING THE LESSON
Place Transparency 14 on the overhead, covering the bottom picture. Point out the triangle and write 11 in the heavy circle at the base of the triangle. Write 4 in one of the other circles, and 7 in the third one. Explain that the number 11 in the dark circle represents the *total* and the numbers in the other circles represent the *parts*. Show students that if you cover one of the numbers, say the 4, they should be able to tell what the covered number is just by looking at the other two numbers. That is, 7 and 4 make 11, the total, so the covered number must be 4.

Erase these numbers. Then, out of view of the students, write 12 in the dark circle and 7 and 5 at the other corners of the triangle. Cover the 5 before showing the display to the students. Ask them what the covered number must be.

Continue the activity with these sets of numbers:

6, 8, and 14	5, 6, and 11
9, 7, and 16	5, 5, and 10
8, 5, and 13	3, 8, and 11

Always write the total in the heavy circle. In most cases cover one of the parts, but occasionally cover the total.

For more practice, repeat with the same sets of numbers, covering the other part.

EXTENDING THE LESSON
To extend the same principle to two-step problems, use the quadrilateral at the bottom of the transparency. The total is still located in the dark circle at the base, but now *three* parts that add together to make the total are located in the other circles. Out of view of the students, write 15 in the dark total circle and 4, 5, and 6 in the other circles. Cover one of the parts and have the students write what the covered number is. If necessary, model for students how to think it through. For example, if you covered the 5, you might think, "6 and 4 make 10, and 10 and 5 make 15, so the covered number must be a 5."

Repeat with the following sets of numbers (always place the largest number, or total, in the dark circle): 2, 5, 6, and 13; 3, 6, 7, and 16; 1, 5, 9, and 15; 8, 4, 3, and 15; 4, 4, 6, and 14.

Continue as needed for practice, using the same sets of numbers but covering a different part each time.

ORAL FOLLOW-UP
Declare a "total of the day," such as 13. Throughout the day, periodically give a student a number that is a part of 13. That student must respond with the number that, when added to the given number, makes the total of the day. Do this with a new total each day for a week.

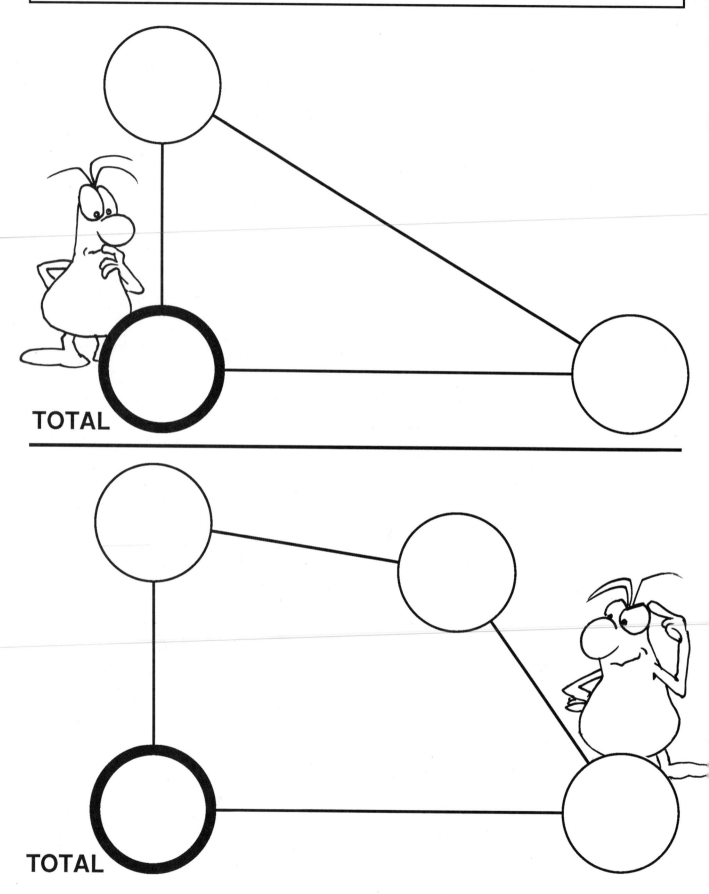

TOTAL

TOTAL

Lesson 15   Thinking Addition

ABOUT THE LESSON
Building on the preceding three lessons, this lesson demonstrates how we can use addition facts that we know to find the answers to subtraction combinations that we do *not* know.

One important aspect of this lesson is the use of the terminology *part, part,* and *total*. These terms have been introduced in the preceding lessons, along with the term "missing part." In the addition fact $6 + 7 = 13$, 6 and 7 are *parts* and 13 is the *total*. In the related subtraction fact $13 - 7 = 6$, 13 is the *total* and 7 and 6 are the *parts*. Thus, in the subtraction combination $14 - 6$, we know one part and the total. With the "think addition" strategy, students will be able to look at a subtraction combination like $14 - 6$, think "6 plus what equals 14?," and determine the missing part.

YOU WILL NEED . . .
• Transparency 15, "Thinking Addition"
• Power Builder 8, page 96

TEACHING THE LESSON
Place Transparency 15 on the overhead, covering all but the top section. Discuss the top picture, where the addition fact $7 + 5 = 12$ is related to subtraction facts that use the same three numbers: $12 - 5 = 7$ and $12 - 7 = 5$. Point out that in an addition fact, *part* plus *part* equals *total,* whereas in a subtraction fact, *total* minus *part* equals *part.* If you know both parts and the total, you can write an addition fact and two subtraction facts.

Uncover the middle of the transparency and write the numbers 8, 6, and 14 in the boxes at the left. Ask the students to name two subtraction facts that have the same parts and total as $8 + 6 = 14$, and write their answers in the boxes at right. Then erase and repeat with such problems as $4 + 7$, $9 + 7$, $4 + 8$, $6 + 5$, and $6 + 9$.

Once students see the relationship between addition and subtraction facts, the next step is to see the same relationship when there is a "missing part." Present the incomplete facts at the bottom of the transparency and ask students to determine the missing part in both facts, thinking "5 plus what equals 13?"

Continue to present incomplete subtraction facts, having students find the missing part in each by "thinking addition." For example:

$10 - 4 = \_\_$	(4 plus what equals 10?)
$15 - 6 = \_\_$	(6 plus what equals 15?)
$13 - 7 = \_\_$	(7 plus what equals 13?)
$16 - 8 = \_\_$	(8 plus what equals 16?)

ORAL FOLLOW-UP
1. Announce that you will state a part and a total. The students must determine the other part and write a subtraction fact using the total and the two parts. For example:

Total 12, part 6. (other part 6; $12 - 6 = 6$)
Total 14, part 7. (other part 7; $14 - 7 = 7$)
Total 11, part 6. (other part 5; $11 - 6 = 5$)
Part 8, total 16. (other part 8; $16 - 8 = 8$)
Part 5, total 12. (other part 7; $12 - 5 = 7$)

Repeat with other parts and totals.

2. Present the following subtraction word problems. Remind students to think addition.

• Brenda had 7 colored pens. Henri gave her some more because he liked her. Then Brenda had 12 pens. How many pens did he give her? (5 pens)

• Matt has 14 balloons for his party. Nine are blue and the rest are red. How many are red? (5 balloons)

• The third grade class at Harrison was collecting milk cartons for recycling. Pete had already collected 8 cartons when Annie's mother gave him some more. Now Pete has 15 cartons. How many did Annie's mother give him? (7 cartons)

• Iris had 12 unshelled peanuts. She shared them with Edie and had 5 left for herself. How many peanuts did she give Edie? (7 peanuts)

• When comparing T-shirts, Steven found out he had 6 more than Carl, who had 9. How many T-shirts did Steven have? (15 T-shirts)

• One windy day Trent was taking 13 perfect papers home from school. He dropped his math book and when he stooped to pick it up, 5 of his papers blew into Lake Grandy and sank. How many perfect papers did Trent get to show his parents? (8 papers)

INDIVIDUAL PRACTICE
Distribute copies of Power Builder 8 for more practice in thinking addition to subtract.

Lesson 16   Using "Make Ten" Combinations

ABOUT THE LESSON

Prior to this lesson, plan to review the concepts presented in lesson 6 (making ten) and lesson 7 (adding ten to a one-digit number). Students should be able to do both easily and quickly.

This lesson presents a way for students to approach subtraction through addition: by starting with the part, adding on to make ten, then adding whatever more is needed to make the total. By keeping track of how much is added on altogether, students determine the answer to the subtraction fact.

This strategy involves more steps than simply thinking addition, but it offers help to students when they don't know the related addition fact. Furthermore, it is a useful strategy that can be applied to subtraction of larger numbers, as will be shown in lesson 17.

YOU WILL NEED . . .
- Transparency 16, "Make Ten . . . and Then Some"
- Transparency 6, "Ten-Frame" (optional)
- Counters
- Power Builder 9, page 97

TEACHING THE LESSON

Place Transparency 16 on the overhead, covering the section at the bottom. Call attention to the subtraction combination $14 - 8$ and explain that to subtract this, we can think of it in terms of an incomplete addition fact, 8 plus what equals 14.

Then demonstrate another way of solving this probem, in two steps. Place 8 counters in the ten-frame and say, "We start with the part, 8, and add to make ten. How many counters do we need to make ten? (2) How many more do we need to make the total, 14? (4) We need 2, then 4 more, so how many are needed in all? (6) The missing part is 6, so $14 - 8 = 6$."

Uncover the problems at the bottom of the transparency. Lead students through each one, using counters in the ten-frame above. Ask them to do the problems by adding to make ten, then adding more to make the total.

For further practice, continue to use counters with the ten-frame above (or the larger one on transparency 6), and repeat the procedure with such subtraction combinations as $15 - 9$, $13 - 5$, and $12 - 7$.

EXTENDING THE LESSON

Put aside the visual model and extend the lesson to a symbolic level by presenting some problems in the following format:

Give a part and a total to the students. Have them add to the part to make ten, then add on to make the total. Ask them how many they added in all. Then ask them to state and answer the related subtraction combination. For example:

YOU SAY: The part is 6 (pause), the total is 14.
STUDENT ANSWERS: 6 plus 4 is 10, plus 4 is 14. I added on 8 in all. So, $14 - 6 = 8$

  The part is 5 (pause), the total is 12.
  (5 plus 5 is 10, plus 2 is 12. Added on 7; $12 - 5 = 7$)

  The part is 7 (pause), the total is 13.
  (7 plus 3 is 10, plus 3 is 13. Added on 6; $13 - 7 = 6$)

  The part is 9 (pause), the total is 16.
  (9 plus 1 is 10, plus 6 is 16. Added on 7; $16 - 9 = 7$)

  The part is 8 (pause), the total is 13.
  (8 plus 2 is 10, plus 3 is 13. Added on 5; $13 - 8 = 5$)

  The part is 4 (pause), the total is 11.
  (4 plus 6 is 10, plus 1 is 11. Added on 7; $11 - 4 = 7$)

Continue with other parts and totals.

ORAL FOLLOW-UP

Present subtraction combinations like those listed below. Tell students to start with the part, add to make ten, add more to make the total, and give the answer.

  $13 - 7$ $(7 + 3 = 10, + 3 = 13,$ answer 6)
  $12 - 8$ $(8 + 2 = 10, + 2 = 12,$ answer 4)
  $11 - 7$ $(7 + 3 = 10, + 1 = 11,$ answer 4)
  $12 - 7$ $(7 + 3 = 10, + 2 = 12,$ answer 5)
  $16 - 9$ $(9 + 1 = 10, + 6 = 16,$ answer 7)
  $14 - 9$ $(9 + 1 = 10, + 4 = 14,$ answer 5)
  $13 - 9$ $(9 + 1 = 10, + 3 = 13,$ answer 4)
  $15 - 9$ $(9 + 1 = 10, + 5 = 15,$ answer 6)

INDIVIDUAL PRACTICE

Distribute copies of Power Builder 9 for more practice in using "make ten" combinations to subtract.

$14 - 8$

To subtract this, think . . .

$8 + \boxed{?} = 14$

How many more are needed to make 14?

You can think of it this way . . .

• Start with the part.

• Add on to make 10.

• Now add on to the total.

• How many in all?

Now you try it. Use the ten-frame.

$14 - 7$ $14 - 5$

$15 - 9$ $13 - 6$

ABOUT THE LESSON

This is an extension of the previous lesson, in which students used "make ten" combinations to help in subtraction. Here the strategy is used with larger numbers.

If the students know how to find the answer to $12 - 7$ by adding to make ten, they should also be able to find the answer to $22 - 17$ in their heads by adding to make a multiple of ten in much the same way. That is, they can think: "$17 + 3 = 20$, and 2 more make 22, so $17 + 5 = 22$, and $22 - 17 = 5$."

YOU WILL NEED . . .

• Transparency 17, "Make Tens to Subtract"

TEACHING THE LESSON

Place Transparency 17 on the overhead, covering all but the top left section. Ask the students to tell how we can find the answer to $12 - 7$ by adding to make 10. (7 plus **3** is 10, and **2** more make 12, and $3 + 2 = 5$, so $12 - 7 = 5$)

Next uncover the top right section of the transparency and explain that we can use the same idea to find the answer to $22 - 17$. Point out the two frames containing a total of 17 dots. Ask:

How many more are needed to fill in the second ten-frame? (3)

That's 20; then how many more are needed to make 22? (2)

How many in all did we add to 17 to make 22? ($3 + 2 = 5$)

So, what's the answer to $22 - 17$? (5)

Uncover the bottom of the transparency. Call on volunteers to explain how we can use "making ten" to find the answer to each of these problems.

Give guidance as necessary, leading students through the same procedure outlined previously.

EXTENDING THE LESSON

Extend this lesson to a more abstract level by presenting subtraction combinations without the visual model of the ten-frame. First present the part, then the total. Ask the students to find the missing part by adding to make ten, then adding on to the total. Finally have them state the complete subtraction fact. For example:

YOU SAY: Part is 34 (pause), total is 42.
STUDENTS THINK: 34 and **6** make 40 and **2** more make 42, so 8 is added to 34. The subtraction fact would be $42 - 34 = 8$.

Part is 23 (pause), total is 31.
(missing part = 8; $31 - 23 = 8$)
Part is 37 (pause), total is 46.
(missing part = 9; $46 - 37 = 9$)
Part is 42 (pause), total is 51.
(missing part = 9; $51 - 42 = 9$)
Part is 18 (pause), total is 24.
(missing part = 6; $24 - 18 = 6$)
Part is 15 (pause), total is 22.
(missing part = 7; $22 - 15 = 7$)
Part is 54 (pause), total is 62.
(missing part = 8; $62 - 54 = 8$)

ORAL FOLLOW-UP

Present subtraction combinations like those below. Encourage students to make tens first to determine the answer.

$46 - 38$ (8)	$53 - 49$ (4)
$66 - 57$ (9)	$23 - 18$ (5)
$43 - 35$ (8)	$81 - 77$ (4)
$122 - 117$ (5)	$763 - 758$ (5)
$276 - 269$ (7)	$394 - 386$ (8)

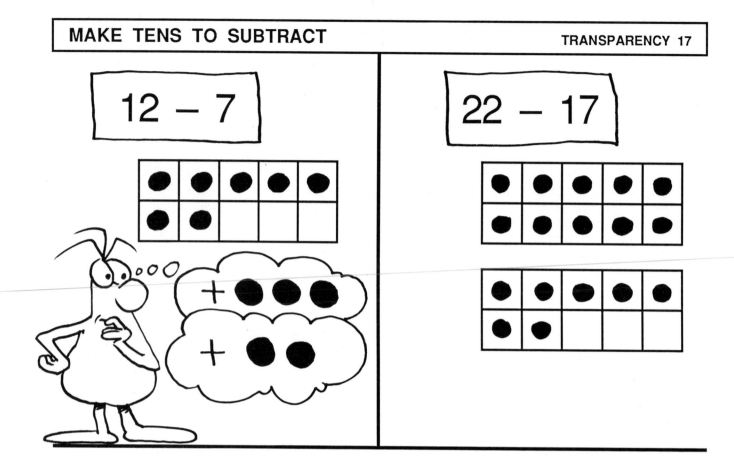

Lesson 18   Using Doubles to Subtract

ABOUT THE LESSON

This lesson introduces the strategy of using the addition double facts to help find the answer to related subtraction combinations. When the part being subtracted is close to half of the total, we can think of an addition double fact (as presented in lesson 3), then adjust as necessary to find the answer.

The problems in this lesson all relate to double facts that need to be adjusted upward by 1 or 2. For example, to find $14 - 6$, we double the 6 to make 12, then adjust by increasing one part (6) by 2 to make 14. So, the answer to $14 - 6$ is $6 + 2$, or 8.

This procedure—double the part, adjust one part to make the right total, and use this adjusted addition fact to solve the subtraction combination—works well for all the subtraction combinations shown in this lesson.

Of course, some students may prefer to do the problems using other mental strategies. Such flexibility and individualization of mental math is to be encouraged, unless the students' alternative strategies are slow or yield incorrect answers.

YOU WILL NEED . . .
- Transparency 18, "Using Doubles to Subtract"
- Power Builders 10 and 11, pages 98–99

TEACHING THE LESSON

Orally present a series of subtraction combinations that directly correspond to addition double facts. For example, present the subtraction combination $10 - 5$. Have students state this in terms of an incomplete addition fact. (5 plus what equals 10?) Ask them what addition double fact we could use to find the answer. ($5 + 5 = 10$) Repeat for $12 - 6$, $14 - 7$, $16 - 8$, and $18 - 9$.

Place Transparency 18 on the overhead, covering the bottom section. Direct attention to the subtraction combination $13 - 6$ and the table of addition double facts. Use $13 - 6$ as an example to show how addition double facts can help us in subtraction. Explain that all we need to do is adjust one part of the double fact to get the right total. That is, since $6 + 6 = 12$, then $6 + 7 = 13$. So we know that the answer to $13 - 6$ is 7.

Ask for a volunteer to explain how the same process works with the second example, $15 - 7$. ($7 + 7 = 14$, so $7 + 8 = 15$, and $15 - 7 = 8$)

Next display the subtraction combinations at the bottom of the transparency. For each one, students should name a double fact and adjust it to find the answer.

EXTENDING THE LESSON

Present subtraction combinations related to more difficult double facts; for example, $25 - 12$, $32 - 15$, $29 - 14$, and $23 - 11$. Ask students to find the answers by using the strategy presented in this lesson—finding a related double and adjusting.

ORAL FOLLOW-UP

Present the following subtraction combinations. Ask students to think of a related addition double fact, adjust it, and then state the answer. (You may also want them to state the double fact they used.

$13 - 6$	($6 + 6 = 12$; answer = 7)
$11 - 5$	($5 + 5 = 10$; answer = 6)
$15 - 7$	($7 + 7 = 14$; answer = 8)
$16 - 7$	($7 + 7 = 14$; answer = 9)
$14 - 6$	($6 + 6 = 12$; answer = 8)
$12 - 6$	($6 + 6 = 12$; answer = 6)
$12 - 5$	($5 + 5 = 10$; answer = 7)
$17 - 8$	($8 + 8 = 16$; answer = 9)

INDIVIDUAL PRACTICE

Distribute copies of Power Builders 10 and 11 for timed mental practice in the basic subtraction facts.

Doubles can help you subtract.

To do this . . .

13 − 6

Think . . .

6 + 6 = 12,
so 6 + **7** = 13 . . .
13 − 6 = 7

4 + 4 = 8

5 + 5 = 10

6 + 6 = 12

7 + 7 = 14

8 + 8 = 16

How does it work with this?

15 − 7

Now you try it.

17 − 8   11 − 5   14 − 6

16 − 7   12 − 5

10 − 4   9 − 4

Unit Two Progress Test

The fifteen-item test below, intended for timed oral presentation, is designed to measure students' mental computation skills in the concepts presented in Unit Two.

Have the students write their names at the top of a sheet of lined paper and number from 1 to 15. Instruct them to write the answer to each problem after the proper number. Emphasize that they will have only 5 seconds to compute the answer in their heads and write it before you go on to the next problem.

Read the problem number, then the problem. Repeat it, wait 5 to 7 seconds, then read the next question.

UNIT TWO TEST	ANSWERS
1. 9 minus 2	1. 7
2. What is 3 less than 7?	2. 4
3. 10 minus 8	3. 2
4. 9 take away 6	4. 3
5. One part is 7. The other part is 5. What is the total?	5. 12
6. The total is 8. One part is 6. What is the other part?	6. 2
7. What would you add to 8 to make 13?	7. 5
8. 9 and what make 15?	8. 6
9. 10 minus 4	9. 6
10. 12 take away 8	10. 4
11. 14 minus 9	11. 5
12. 13 minus 8	12. 5
13. How much greater than 59 is 63?	13. 4
14. 16 minus 8	14. 8
15. 13 minus 6	15. 7

Thinking in Patterns

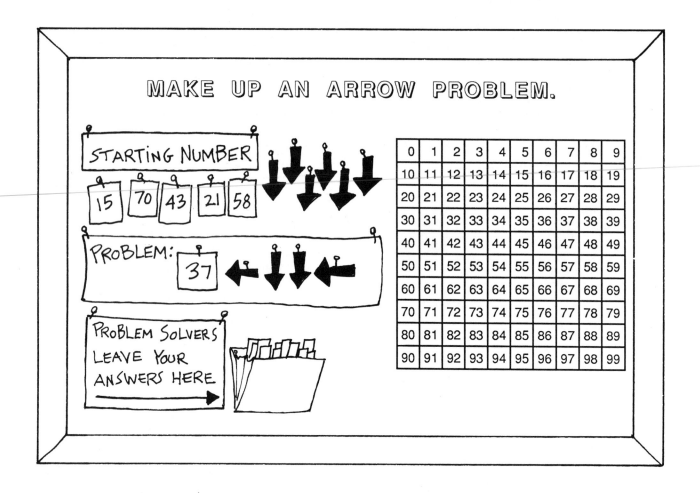

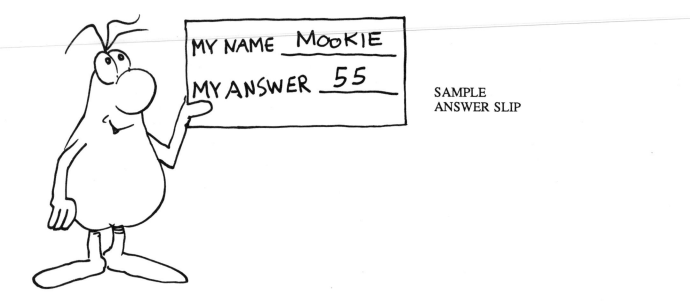

SAMPLE
ANSWER SLIP

UNIT THREE OVERVIEW

As we prepare young students for mental computation, one of the most important prerequisite skills we can teach them is the ability to notice and take advantage of patterns in our base ten system. Another important skill to teach is *flexibility,* showing them that they can apply alternative thinking strategies, depending on the specific numbers and on the operations within a given problem. Those skills are the emphasis of Units Three and Four.

In this unit, students will work with several visual models to help them see the patterns in our number system and to develop mental rather than paper-and-pencil methods for simple calculation. These models include the 100 chart, the ten-frame, and base ten blocks, as well as a more abstract model, the display of a calculator. The patterns developed in this unit involve adding and subtracting 1, 10, and multiples of 10. These patterns form the foundation for the more sophisticated mental computation strategies that are presented in Unit Four. Although an order of presentation is suggested by the numbering of the lessons in this unit, some of the lessons can be interchanged according to your preference. Note, however, that lessons 21–25 (based on the 100 chart) follow a sequence of increasing difficulty.

Make **the 100 chart** a highly visible part of your classroom. It could be the center of an activity-focused bulletin board (as shown opposite). In addition, some students will benefit from having their own 100 chart, which might be laminated onto each student desk or inside a book cover. A blackline master of four small 100 charts that can be cut apart and distributed to students is provided on page 116. NOTE: The 100 chart that we use in this program is actually a 0–99 chart; you may be familiar with similar charts that display the numbers 1–100. We prefer the 0–99 chart because it teaches that zero is an important number and because it yields single digits all the way across the top row.

Base ten blocks, highly recommended for use in elementary mathematics, are available in either plastic or wood from school-supply dealers. If you do not have or cannot obtain them, use the blackline master on page 117 to make a set of ones ("units"), tens ("longs"), and hundreds ("flats") for use with the activities in Units Three and Four.

The activities suggested in this unit will take from 10–15 minutes each. However, most can (and should) be repeated on several different days. Some make good short activities that can be carried on while students are performing routine tasks such as lining up or handing in papers. Because the emphasis is on visual models rather than symbolic problems, there are no Power Builder sets for this unit.

BULLETIN BOARD FOR UNIT THREE

Since the 100 chart is an important model for this unit, consider creating or purchasing a large laminated 100 chart for a central bulletin board. This can be the focus of numerous learning activities; one possibility is illustrated opposite.

For this activity, tack up beside the 100 chart several cardboard arrows, a variety of number squares, and a pocket with blank answer slips. Students are to use any starting number and the arrows to make up a problem that they tack into the problem box. Classmates leave their answers in the pocket.

A NOTE ON CALCULATORS

Hand-held calculators are required for the activities in lessons 19 and 20. For presenting lessons to the group, you may want to obtain a solar powered overhead calculator that can be placed on the overhead projector for whole-class viewing.

Most simple four-function calculators have a built-in feature called the *constant addend.* This feature essentially lets us program the calculator to count. While different calculators have their own keystroking sequence to make this counting possible, most will do it using this sequence:

PRESS 0 + 1 = = = = ...

As you continue to press the equals key without touching any other keys, the display will count up by ones, 0, 1, 2, 3, 4, 5, . . . , until you press CLEAR. What you've instructed the calculator to do is to start at 0 (the first number entered in the sequence) and to add 1 continuously. To count by twos, you would press this sequence: 0 + 2 = = = ... Of course, you could start at any number rather than 0. For example, to start at 3 and count by 10, press 3 + 10 = = = ... You should see the numbers displayed as 13, 23, 33, 43, and so on.

To count backwards, try this:

PRESS 10 − 1 = = = = ...

You should see the numbers displayed as 9, 8, 7, 6, ... To start at any other number, just replace the 10 with your new starting number. To count back by a number other than 1, replace 1 with your constant subtractor.

Remember that some calculators work differently. Before presenting lessons 19 and 20, experiment with the model you have available. Casio brand calculators generally have the same capabilities, but the keystroke sequence is slightly different: you press the constant addend (or subtractor) *first,* then press the operation key (+ or −) *twice,* followed by the starting number and the repeated equals. For example, to start at 10 and count forward by fives, the keystroking sequence is this:

PRESS 5 + + 10 = = = = ...

Lesson 19 Skip Counting by Ones, Twos, and Threes

ABOUT THE LESSON

Calculators are a motivating tool for young students. This lesson and the one that follows capitalize on this motivation as they use the constant addend capability of the calculator to highlight certain patterns in our number system. Recognizing these patterns is important as students learn to deal with numbers mentally. Such patterns help us find and use shortcuts to many arithmetic procedures.

YOU WILL NEED . . .

- Calculators—one for each student, if possible
- An overhead calculator (optional)
- Transparency 19, "Skip Counting Record Sheet" (optional)
- Individual 100 charts, page 116 (optional)

TEACHING THE LESSON

If you have an overhead calculator that allows the whole class to view the display at once, you will probably want to use it with this lesson.

Begin by teaching students the keystroke sequence for counting by 1, starting at 0:

PRESS 0 + 1 = = = . . .*

Have the students carefully key this sequence into their calculators and continue to press the equals key until the display reaches 30. You may want to have students name the numbers aloud as they appear on the display. Next have them count by twos, starting at 0:

PRESS 0 + 2 = = = . . .

Again, have them continue until the display reaches 30. Ask which sequence took longer, counting by *ones* to 30 or by *twos* to 30.

Ask students to predict how long it will take to count to 100 using the calculator. Record their predictions on the board or overhead. Then try this simple race: See who can be the first to reach 100 *without going over 100.* (This will force them to pay attention to the display and notice place value patterns.) Ask everyone to enter just 0 + 1, then wait for you to say *GO.* In most cases it will take students between 20 and 40 seconds to reach 100. Time them and record the best time on the board or on the Transparency 19 record sheet.

---

*Or alternative sequence, depending on the calculator you are using. See page 46 for an extended discussion of the keystroke sequence for counting with the calculator.

Now try a second race. Ask students to predict how long it will take to count to 100 by twos using the calculator. Set them up as before, being sure everyone waits until you say *GO.* Remind students that they must stop exactly at 100. Record the best time. Draw attention to the fact that this race took less time—in fact, about half the time. Pose these questions: "Suppose we had another race, this time counting by threes to 100. About how long do you think it would take? Could we stop exactly at 100?"

Have students key in the sequence for counting back by ones (PRESS 100 – 1 = = = . . .). Point out that it will take them about the same amount of time to count backwards as forwards between 100 and 0. If, when counting back, students go too far (and many will), they will begin to see negative numbers displayed on the calculator. A good model for explaining these numbers is the thermometer; that is, remind students that it is possible for the thermometer to go "below" zero.

Continue these activities, counting forwards and backwards by different numbers. At times, have students orally name numbers as they are displayed, or have them predict what the next number will be. Additionally, for a particular pattern, students might record on a 100 chart the numbers they see on the calculator's display. Colored pencils or markers can be used to highlight different patterns.

EXTENDING THE LESSON

Ask: "How long do you think it would take us to count to 1,000 by ones on the calculator? Could it be done in a minute? an hour? a day? Suppose we counted by tens to 1,000. How long would it take? Try it."

ORAL FOLLOW-UP

A few days after doing this lesson, ask students to talk about some of the patterns they discovered when skip counting on the calculator. For example: "What is common about all the numbers that appear when you skip count by fives? by tens? Which is faster, skip counting by threes or by fives? Why?"

You may want to have some students (or the class as a group) skip count without the aid of the calculator. Students should do such skip counting in association with a realistic problem-solving activity. For example, they should think of such things as pairs of hands as they count by twos, nickels as they count by fives, and so on.

Skip count by 1's to 100.

   How long does it take? _____

Skip count by 2's to 100.

   How long does it take? _____

   What patterns do you notice? _____

_____

_____

Skip count by 3's to 100.

   How long does it take? _____

   What patterns do you notice? _____

_____

_____

Skip count by 5's, then by 10's, to 100.

   How long does each take? _____

   What is alike about each pattern? _____

_____

Predict how long it would take to:

   Count by 1's to 1,000. _____

   Count by 1's to 10,000. _____

   Count by 1's to 100,000. _____

   Count by 1's to 1,000,000. _____

   Count by 10's to 1,000,000. _____

Lesson 20   Skip Counting by Fives, Tens, and Hundreds

ABOUT THE LESSON

Building on the previous lesson, we now use the calculator to generate and verify sequences of numbers whose patterns are fundamental for proficiency at mental computation. In particular, this lesson focuses on the very valuable patterns that occur when we (with or without the calculator) skip count by numbers such as 5, 10, 25, 50, and 100.

YOU WILL NEED . . .
- Calculators for the students
- An overhead calculator (optional)
- Transparency 20, "Skip Counting Pattern Grid"
- Quarters (12 or more), half dollars (6 or more), and dollar bills (several)

TEACHING THE LESSON

As with lesson 19, you might use an overhead calculator to present these activities.

Review the calculator keystroking sequence for skip counting as introduced in the last lesson. (Typically, to count by fives beginning at 0, PRESS 0 + 5 = = = = ...)

Ask students to count by fives on the calculator, beginning at 0 and continuing until they reach 50. Have them name each number aloud as it is displayed. Then have them clear the display and start over. The second time through, they should write on a sheet of paper all the numbers they see. You may want to do this with them on the overhead, using Transparency 20. If you use this grid (which is essentially a blank 100 chart), place each number in its proper position, as shown.

0				5					
10				15					
20				25					
30				35					
40				45					
50									

Ask students what patterns they notice. (Each number ends in either 5 or 0.) You might have students continue this skip counting sequence well past 50 to demonstrate that the pattern continues even for larger numbers.

Repeat the activity for counting by tens. Before turning to the calculator, you might check to see how high students can count by tens on their own. Then have students count on the calculator. Remember that an important part of this lesson is the discussion of any patterns they see while skip counting.

Next, try skip counting by twenty-fives. Ask students to name an everyday model that could help them. (quarters) Display a handful of quarters to demonstrate and reinforce this idea. As students skip count by twenty-fives on the calculator, lay down one quarter for each number, stacking them in groups of four (or $1).

Have students skip count by fifties and by hundreds, following the same process. Use half dollars and dollar bills as visual models.

EXTENDING THE LESSON

Ask students to skip count by fives, beginning at the number 3 (PRESS 3 + 5 = = = . . .). Ask, "Can you predict any pattern? How will this pattern be related to the pattern you saw when you started at 0?" Next have them try skip counting by tens, beginning at 3.

ORAL FOLLOW-UP

A day or two after this lesson, use the following warm-up for your math session. Have the class, in unison, begin counting by fives. Stop them when they reach 35, and direct them to count by tens from that point. Continue in this fashion, stopping them at various points in the sequence to switch from tens to fives and back. Another time you could vary the activity by having students switch back and forth between twenty-fives, fifties, and hundreds.

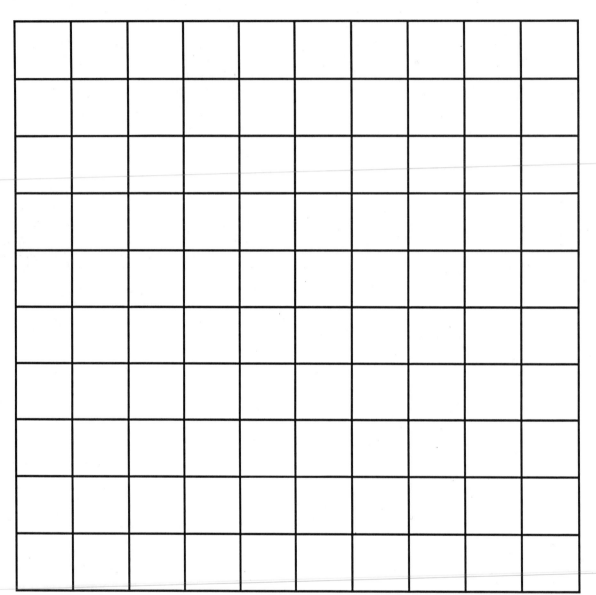

Lesson 21   Patterns on the 100 Chart

ABOUT THE LESSON

In this lesson, students continue their study of patterns in the numbers from 0 to 100, this time with the visual aid of a 100 chart. The 100 chart is an indispensable tool for developing the mental visualization that students need in order to be successful in mental math. It is used in lessons 21–25, as well as in Unit Four, as an aid to mental addition and subtraction. As suggested in the unit overview, you might enlarge the 100 chart and place it prominently in your classroom for reference throughout this unit. Be sure students understand the distinction between *columns* and *rows* on the chart.

The most important objective of this lesson is to show students how our base ten number system is arranged. In particular, students should recognize the repeated use of just ten digits (0 – 9) to name all the numbers.

YOU WILL NEED . . .

• Transparency 21, "Finding Number Patterns"
• "Four 100 Charts," page 116, one full-page copy for each student (optional, for "Extending the Lesson")

TEACHING THE LESSON

Display Transparency 21 on the overhead. Ask, "Why do you think this is called a 100 chart? (It contains 100 numbers.) What can you say about how the numbers are arranged?"

Draw attention to various number patterns apparent on the chart. For example, you might ask:

What's alike about all the numbers in the third *column*? (All have a ones digit of 2.)

What's alike about all the numbers in the fifth *row*? (All have a tens digit of 4.)

Can you locate—with just your eyes—all the numbers whose tens and ones digits are the same? What can you tell us about where they are? (They lie along a diagonal through the center of the chart, from top left to bottom right.)

Does 0 fit this pattern? (Although it doesn't seem to, it really does; we could write 0 as 00, meaning no tens and no ones.)

Look at all the numbers along the other diagonal—from top right to bottom left. Can you find a pattern in these numbers? (Starting at top right and moving down, as the ones digit *decreases* by one, the tens digit *increases* by one. Also, for every number on this diagonal, the sum of both digits is 9.)

Ask students to find and describe other patterns in the chart. If they need help getting started, suggest that they find all the numbers with a ones digit that is one less than the tens digit (such as 21 or 98). Ask, "What pattern is formed by these numbers? (a diagonal)"

To emphasize the oral as well as the visual patterns in the chart, have students start at the top of one column (or the beginning of one row) and name all the numbers in that column (or row). Next, have them start at the bottom of a column or the end of a row and work backwards to name all the numbers.

Eventually, ask them to name these numbers without looking at the chart; this encourages them to form mental images of the patterns they have been observing.

EXTENDING THE LESSON

Give each student a copy of "Four 100 Charts" (page 116). On chart 1, have them start at 0, skip count by twos, and color each number they count. (They will be coloring 0, 2, 4, 6, and so on.) Ask them to describe the pictured pattern.

For chart 2, ask students to predict the pattern if they color every *third* number, beginning with 0. Then have them do it and describe the pattern they create.

Use charts 3 and 4 to continue predicting, counting, coloring, and describing number patterns. You might have students count by fours and fives, or possibly by nines and elevens.

ORAL FOLLOW-UP

To encourage using patterns for prediction, cover the location of several numbers on Transparency 21. (Small Post-it notes work nicely for this activity.) Place the transparency on the overhead and ask students to identify the hidden numbers.

0	1	2	3	4	5	6	7	8	9
10	11	12	13	14	15	16	17	18	19
20	21	22	23	24	25	26	27	28	29
30	31	32	33	34	35	36	37	38	39
40	41	42	43	44	45	46	47	48	49
50	51	52	53	54	55	56	57	58	59
60	61	62	63	64	65	66	67	68	69
70	71	72	73	74	75	76	77	78	79
80	81	82	83	84	85	86	87	88	89
90	91	92	93	94	95	96	97	98	99

100 CHART

Lesson 22   Tracing Paths on the 100 Chart

ABOUT THE LESSON

This lesson reinforces patterns in the base ten number system as students learn to move around mentally on the 100 chart. The very act of mentally and visually following described paths is an important and useful technique in mental computation.

Students generally get very involved in this activity. Some are more adept from the start at tracing the paths described without having the 100 chart before their eyes. However, with a little practice, most of your students will be able to follow these paths entirely in their minds.

YOU WILL NEED . . .
- Transparency 22, "Tracing Paths"
- Individual 100 charts (Duplicate and cut apart the small 100 charts on page 116; give one to each student.)

TEACHING THE LESSON

Remind students of some of the number patterns they have noticed and described on the 100 chart (as discussed in lesson 21). Place Transparency 22 on the overhead and cover the bottom section. Use a blank sheet of paper to cover all but the first row and column of the 100 chart.

Call on a student to go to the chart (as projected on the wall or screen) and point to where he or she thinks a particular number, such as 25, is located. Once the student has guessed, remove the cover from the chart to check. Continue this activity with various numbers until the students demonstrate a good grasp of the layout of the chart.

Next, give each student an individual copy of the 100 chart. Explain that you are going to give them some paths to follow from a starting number, and that they must tell you the ending

number. As you give directions, they are to use a finger or the *eraser* end of a pencil to trace an invisible path along the chart. Start with fairly simple paths. For example:

Find 25 on the chart—that's the starting number. Go down one block, down one more block, now up one block. What number are you on? (35)

Start at 25 again. Go up one block, to the right one block, down one block, down one more block. What number are you on? (36)

Start at 25. Go down two blocks, to the left one block, up one block, down three blocks. What number are you on? (64)

Continue these paths as long as students seem interested. Then have them put the individual 100 charts away and look again at the transparency. Read them the sets of directions under the chart while they trace each path with only their eyes. Once students can do this successfully, remove the transparency and ask them to follow some simple paths in their minds, without looking at the 100 chart at all. For example:

Think of 35, go down one block; where are you? (45)

Think of 77. Go up one block, then right one block. Where are you? (68)

EXTENDING THE LESSON

1. Give increasingly longer paths for students to trace without looking at the 100 chart. For example:

Start at 34. Go down one block, down another block, up one block, to the right one block, down one block, to the right one block, up one block.

2. Ask students to make up paths and to describe them orally to other members of the class. Each student describing a path must be able to give the correct ending number.

ORAL FOLLOW-UP

With all 100 charts out of view, ask questions about the arrangement of numbers on the chart. For example:

What number is just below 26? (36)
What number is just below 80? (90)
What number is just above 14? (4)
What number is just to the left of 47? (46)

0	1	2	3	4	5	6	7	8	9
10	11	12	13	14	15	16	17	18	19
20	21	22	23	24	25	26	27	28	29
30	31	32	33	34	35	36	37	38	39
40	41	42	43	44	45	46	47	48	49
50	51	52	53	54	55	56	57	58	59
60	61	62	63	64	65	66	67	68	69
70	71	72	73	74	75	76	77	78	79
80	81	82	83	84	85	86	87	88	89
90	91	92	93	94	95	96	97	98	99

1. Start at 53. Go . . .
   down 2 blocks,
   right 3 blocks.
   Where are you?

2. Start at 61. Go . . .
   right 2 blocks,
   up 2 blocks.
   Where are you?

3. Start at 47. Go . . .
   down 1 block,
   up 2 blocks,
   left 1 block.
   Where are you?

4. Start at 72. Go . . .
   up 4 blocks,
   right 3 blocks,
   left 1 block.
   Where are you?

Lesson 23   Arrow Moves on the 100 Chart

ABOUT THE LESSON
This lesson extends the previous one by introducing written notation (arrows) to represent movement on the 100 chart.

YOU WILL NEED . . .
• Transparency 23, "Arrow Moves"
• Individual 100 charts (optional)

TEACHING THE LESSON
Remind students of the mental maneuvering they have done on the 100 chart, following different paths in their minds (as presented in lesson 22). For review, tell them to think of where the number 19 is on the chart. Then ask, "What number is two blocks below it? (39) Four blocks below it? (59) One block below and three blocks to the left of it? (26)"

Explain that you are going to show them an easy way to describe, in writing, such mental moves on the chart. Place Transparency 23 on the overhead and focus attention on the notation 19 ↓↓ . Ask students what they think it directs them to do. (Start at 19 and go down one block, then down another block to reach 39.)

Continue this activity with the other arrow moves on the transparency. Present additional paths as needed to provide adequate practice and reinforce the patterns. Use a variety of different starting numbers.

Once students have a good grasp of arrow moves, you might introduce the idea of taking "shortcuts" to arrive at each answer. For example, we can think of the first two arrows in this path as canceling each other out:

$$43 \rightarrow \leftarrow \uparrow \uparrow \downarrow$$

Likewise, the last two arrows cancel each other out, leaving only 43 ↑, or 33. This is a nice application of inverse operations that will benefit many students.

If time permits, give students a "start" and "stop" number and have them fill in appropriate arrows. Encourage discussion of the fact that there is more than one way to do any such problem. At some stage, you may want to challenge students to fill in as few arrows as possible between the numbers.

EXTENDING THE LESSON
For those students who are ready for the challenge, introduce diagonal arrows (↘ ↙ ↗ ↖). Ask students to picture their mental 100 chart and predict what the move 42 ↘ would produce. Continue with other examples.

ORAL FOLLOW-UP
Provide two numbers, such as 56 and 45. Ask the students to describe different patterns (arrow moves) to connect these numbers.

0	1	2	3	4	5	6	7	8	9
10	11	12	13	14	15	16	17	18	19
20	21	22	23	24	25	26	27	28	29
30	31	32	33	34	35	36	37	38	39
40	41	42	43	44	45	46	47	48	49
50	51	52	53	54	55	56	57	58	59
60	61	62	63	64	65	66	67	68	69
70	71	72	73	74	75	76	77	78	79
80	81	82	83	84	85	86	87	88	89
90	91	92	93	94	95	96	97	98	99

Make these moves.
Where do you end up?

19 ↓ ↓

19 ↓ ↓ ← ← ↑

19 ↓ ↑ ← ← ← →

24 ↓ ↓ ← ← ↑

36 ↓ → → →

43 → ← ↑ ↑ ↓

Lesson 24   Using the 100 Chart to Add and Subtract Tens and Ones

ABOUT THE LESSON
The preceding three lessons have encouraged students to study and use the patterns of our base ten system to make mental moves on the 100 chart. This lesson introduces what those moves mean mathematically; for example, "down one block" means "add ten."

YOU WILL NEED . . .
• Transparency 24, "Add and Subtract on the 100 Chart"
• Individual 100 charts

TEACHING THE LESSON
Place Transparency 24 on the overhead. Remind students that we can use arrows (↓↑→←) to represent movements from any given numbered block to another. Focus attention on the four problems in row number 1 on the transparency. As students complete the problems, write their answers in the blanks. Then ask, "What mathematical operation can we use to represent the down arrow?" (We are adding 10, so ↓ means +10.)

Do the same thing with rows 2, 3, and 4, each time leading students to define the meaning of the directional arrow. (↑ means –10; → means +1; ← means –1.) Review by filling in the bottom of the transparency.

EXTENDING THE LESSON
Display a problem such as 43 ↓↓→ . Ask students to rewrite the problem *without using the arrows*. For example, 43 ↓↓→ could be written as 43 + 10 + 10 + 1. You might have students calculate the answer as well, one step at a time. That is, "Start at 43, then 53, 63, 64."

ORAL FOLLOW-UP
Give the following problems orally, reading each one slowly. Have students write their answers on paper. Allow them to use their individual 100 charts initially, but repeat the exercise later without the chart.

$26 + 10 + 10 + 10$ (56)
$34 + 10 + 1$ (45)
$55 + 10 + 1 + 1 + 1$ (68)
$43 + 10 - 10 - 10 + 1$ (34)
$26 - 10 - 10 + 10$ (16)

Make these moves
on the chart.
Where do you end up?

0	1	2	3	4	5	6	7	8	9
10	11	12	13	14	15	16	17	18	19
20	21	22	23	24	25	26	27	28	29
30	31	32	33	34	35	36	37	38	39
40	41	42	43	44	45	46	47	48	49
50	51	52	53	54	55	56	57	58	59
60	61	62	63	64	65	66	67	68	69
70	71	72	73	74	75	76	77	78	79
80	81	82	83	84	85	86	87	88	89
90	91	92	93	94	95	96	97	98	99

1. 45 ↓ ___   36 ↓ ___   53 ↓ ___   81 ↓ ___

2. 45 ↑ ___   36 ↑ ___   53 ↑ ___   81 ↑ ___

3. 45 → ___   36 → ___   53 → ___   81 → ___

3. 45 ← ___   36 ← ___   53 ← ___   81 ← ___

↓ means _____

↑ means _____

→ means _____

← means _____

Lesson 25   Using the 100 Chart to Add and Subtract Multiples of Ten

ABOUT THE LESSON
Lessons in Unit Four will use base ten blocks to introduce techniques for mentally adding and subtracting multiples of ten. This lesson builds a foundation for that work through further use of arrow movement on the 100 chart.

YOU WILL NEED . . .
• Transparency 25, "Arrow Math" (optional)
• Individual 100 charts

TEACHING THE LESSON
Write the problem 26 ↓↓↓ on the board and ask students for the answer. (56) Give several more such problems (problems that use multiple vertical arrows of the same type, either up or down). For example:

35 ↑↑ (15)
43 ↓↓↓ (73)
52 ↓↓↓↓ (92)
59 ↑↑↑↑↑ (9)
78 ↑↑ (58)

As students give each answer, ask them to find a "short way" to express each problem in math language. If necessary, have them write the problem out the "long way" first, using a +10 or −10 for each arrow. (You might use Transparency 25 on the overhead to organize this discussion, or simply present it at the board.) Make up additional problems as needed until students have the idea.

Next, write the following "short form" problems on the board. Suggest that students can use their 100 charts to solve these. For example, for the first problem, students would look at 45 and drop down three blocks.

45 + 30   (75)
73 − 20   (53)
52 + 40   (92)
86 − 10   (76)
53 + 30   (83)
98 − 70   (28)

While some students will still rely on the 100 chart to solve such problems, others may already be working completely mentally.

When students have finished these problems, write their answers on the board. Have them look at each problem and answer and describe any patterns they notice (for example, the ones digit always remains the same).

EXTENDING THE LESSON
For students who catch on very quickly, introduce a second step to each of the problems in the lesson, using only vertical arrows (+10 or −10). For example:

43 ↓↓↓ ↑↑, or 43 + 30 − 20

ORAL FOLLOW-UP
Present the following questions orally. Ask students to use their mental 100 charts (without looking at an actual chart) to answer each one.

Start at 23. Go down 3 blocks. Where are you? (53)

Start at 86. Go up 2 blocks. Where are you? (66)

Start at 49. Go down 4 blocks. Where are you? (89)

Start at 98. Go up 5 blocks. Where are you? (48)

0	1	2	3	4	5	6	7	8	9
10	11	12	13	14	15	16	17	18	19
20	21	22	23	24	25	26	27	28	29
30	31	32	33	34	35	36	37	38	39
40	41	42	43	44	45	46	47	48	49
50	51	52	53	54	55	56	57	58	59
60	61	62	63	64	65	66	67	68	69
70	71	72	73	74	75	76	77	78	79
80	81	82	83	84	85	86	87	88	89
90	91	92	93	94	95	96	97	98	99

ARROW MATH PROBLEM	WRITTEN WITH OPERATION SYMBOLS	WRITTEN IN SHORT FORM
35 ↑↑	$35 - 10 - 10 =$	$35 - 20 =$
43 ↓↓↓		
52 ↓↓↓↓		
59 ↓↓↓↓↓		
78 ↑↑		

Lesson 26   Chaining Operations with One-Digit Numbers

ABOUT THE LESSON

This lesson offers students a chance to review basic facts at the same time they are learning to do multistep problems in their heads. To establish the mental process in this lesson, you will be presenting problems orally while using the ten-frame and counters for visual support.

YOU WILL NEED . . .
• Transparency 26, "Number Chains"
• Counters

TEACHING THE LESSON

Place Transparency 26 on the overhead, covering the problems at the bottom. Remind students of the ten-frame they used in lesson 6. Lay 8 counters in the frame and ask how many there are. Then remove 2 counters, describing what you are doing: "I'll take away 2, now how many are there?" (6)

Next add 3 more counters, again describing the action and asking students to tell how many are in the ten-frame. Continue adding and subtracting counters in this way, keeping each answer somewhere between 0 and 10.

Repeat the activity with several such chain problems, each containing four to six steps.

Now do another chain problem with counters in the ten-frame, but this time write (on the overhead or the board) the number sentence for the problem you have created. Write each step as you do it with the counters. When the problem is finished, your written record might look like this:

$$8 + 1 - 4 + 3 - 2 - 1 = 5$$

At this point, students should be ready to do these same problems without using the counters. Without displaying to the class the problems at the bottom of the transparency, read each problem aloud, one step at a time, going slowly. After students have written their answers to the problem, expose it on the transparency and ask one student to work it aloud.

EXTENDING THE LESSON

In the next lesson, students will be doing chain problems with two-digit numbers. To extend the present lesson, you might include facts through 18. You could use longer chains and incorporate simple multiplication or division steps as well. For example:

Start at 2. Multiply by 3. Add 1. Subtract 2. Divide by 5. Add 1. What number is left? (2)

ORAL FOLLOW-UP

Allow students to use their fingers as a built in ten-frame while you orally give them a number of chain problems. For example:

Start with 9. Subtract 2. Add 1. Subtract 3. Subtract 2. Add 2. What number is left? (5)

1. $5 + 3 - 4 + 3 - 5 =$

2. $3 + 1 + 5 - 5 + 5 =$

3. $5 - 4 + 3 + 6 - 1 - 6 =$

4. $3 + 7 - 4 + 2 - 6 + 1 =$

5. $8 - 4 - 2 - 1 + 5 + 3 - 3 =$

Lesson 27　Chaining Operations with One- and Two-Digit Numbers

ABOUT THE LESSON

Building on their work in the preceding lesson, students here practice doing mental number chains with one- and two-digit numbers. The concrete model they will use, base ten blocks, is probably a familiar one. If you do not have wooden or plastic base ten blocks, use the blackline master on page 117 to make a small set of tagboard blocks for each student.

YOU WILL NEED . . .

• Base ten blocks (units and longs)
• Transparency 27, "Using Base Ten Blocks"

TEACHING THE LESSON

Place Transparency 27 on the overhead as a base for this lesson's work. In the large counting space on the transparency, lay out 4 tens and 5 ones using base ten blocks. Ask students to name the number represented. (45)

Remove the blocks, but then put them back on the transparency, laying down each piece one at a time. Lay down the longs first, followed by the units. Ask students to name the number that is represented at each step. Students will be verbalizing this sequence: 10, 20, 30, 40, 41, 42, 43, 44, 45.

Now remove the blocks and again lay them down one at a time, this time beginning with the units, followed by the longs. Again, have students name each number represented at each step. (1, 2, 3, 4, 5, 15, 25, 35, 45)

Pick up the blocks once again and again lay them down one piece at a time—this time *randomly*. Have students name the number represented at each step. (The sequence will vary; one possible sequence would be as follows: 1, 2, 12, 13, 23, 33, 34, 44, 45.)

Point out that all this time, the total number and type of blocks used never changed, only the order in which you laid them down.

Use the same blocks to model subtracting by ones and tens. Start by again laying out 45 on the transparency. Then take away one block at a time, asking students to name the number displayed at each step.

Turn off the overhead projector and give each student or pair of students 9 longs and 9 units. Explain that they are going to work chain problems with these base ten blocks. Tell them to follow your directions as you give step-by-step chain problems. Use problems similar to those you created for the ten-frame in lesson 26, but including both tens and ones. For example:

> Start with 2 tens 3 ones. What number is this? (23)
>
> Add 1 ten. What number is this? (33)
>
> Add 3 ones. What number is this? (36)
>
> Take away 2 tens. What number is this? (16)

Continue with oral problems of this type as long as students remain interested and engaged.

At some point, you might begin symbolizing some of the problems on the board or overhead, following the general sequence illustrated in the box at the bottom of this page.

When you think students are ready, ask them to try several problems without using the base ten models. For example:

> Start with 25. Add 20. Subtract 1. What number is left? (44)

ORAL FOLLOW-UP

Give students oral work with chain problems like the following:

$30 + 20 + 3 - 10 + 1$　(44)
$40 + 2 - 20 + 10$　(32)
$53 + 10 - 20 + 1$　(44)
$21 - 10 + 3 - 2 + 30$　(42)
$93 - 20 - 1 - 40 + 1$　(33)

SEQUENCE TO DEMONSTRATE SYMBOLIZING CHAIN PROBLEMS			
YOU SAY	STUDENTS LAY DOWN	STUDENTS SAY	YOU WRITE
Start with 23.		23	23
Add 2 tens.		43	$23 + 20$
Subtract one.		42	$23 + 20 - 1$

Unit Three Progress Test

The fifteen-item test below, intended for timed oral presentation, is designed to measure students' mental computation skills in the concepts presented in Unit Three.

Have the students write their names at the top of a sheet of lined paper and number from 1 to 15. Instruct them to write the answer to each problem after the proper number. Emphasize that they will have only 5 seconds to compute the answer in their heads and write it before you go on to the next problem.

Read the problem number, then the problem. Repeat it, wait 5 to 7 seconds, then read the next question.

UNIT THREE TEST	ANSWERS
1. What number comes next: 22, 24, 26 . . . ?	1. 28
2. What is the next number: 3, 6, 9 . . . ?	2. 12
3. What comes next: 25, 30, 35 . . . ?	3. 40
4. What number is one right of 45 on the 100 chart?	4. 46
5. What number is just below 68 on the 100 chart?	5. 78
6. What does an arrow pointing to the left mean?	6. − 1
7. What does an arrow pointing down mean?	7. + 10
8. 45 plus 10 plus 10	8. 65
9. 63 minus 10 minus 10	9. 43
10. 30 plus 50	10. 80
11. What is 40 more than 20?	11. 60
12. 90 minus 30	12. 60
13. What is 60 less than 90?	13. 30
14. Start at 4. Add 2. Subtract 3. Add 8. What is the answer?	14. 11
15. Start at 34. Add 20. Subtract 3. Subtract 10. What is the answer?	15. 41

Thinking Strategies for Larger Numbers

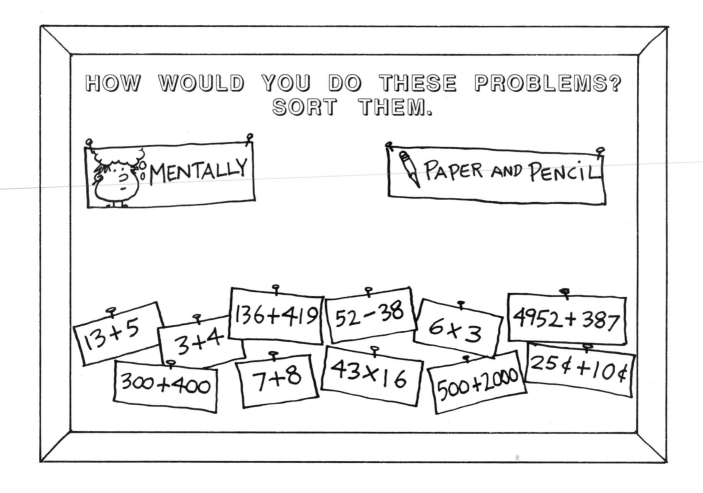

UNIT FOUR OVERVIEW

In using Units One and Two of this book, you taught your students thinking strategies for dealing with basic addition and subtraction combinations. In Unit Three, the emphasis was on important place value concepts. In particular, students used a variety of visual models to help them see clearly the important patterns in our base ten number system.

All this earlier work has formed the foundation for the final unit of *Mental Math in the Primary Grades*. In this last unit, you will expose your students to some simple techniques for mentally computing multidigit addition and subtraction problems. Problems that involve a multiple of ten as an addend receive the most emphasis. A few more sophisticated strategies involving numbers that are *near* multiples of ten (such as 9, 19, 29) will be developed in the later lessons of this unit.

One of the goals of this unit is to lead students from working in their heads with visual models to being able to mentally compute problems stated symbolically. To help meet this goal, most lessons include two standard features. The first is a set of "TRY THESE IN YOUR HEAD" practice problems at the bottom of the teaching transparency; the second is a reproducible Power Builder page for individual practice.

The TRY THESE exercises are to be used only as needed, and should be viewed as an extension of the instruction. Do them orally with the students, pausing with each one to discuss students' answers and their methods of solution.

The Power Builder sets each present twenty standard arithmetic problems for students to do in their heads. Each problem set mirrors the thinking strategy taught in the corresponding lesson. You might use these Power Builders either immediately following the lesson or several days later as a form of review. Work on the Power Builders should be timed to encourage quick mental computation.

BULLETIN BOARD FOR UNIT FOUR

One of the important teaching goals of this book is to help students become aware of not only **how** to mentally compute, but also **when** to do a problem mentally rather than with paper and pencil. The suggested bulletin board (illustrated opposite) allows students to compare a variety of problems and discuss which ones might be easily done with mental computation.

Place an assortment of index cards on bulletin board with tacks so that students can move them. On each card, print a problem appropriate for the abilities of your students—some being obvious candidates for mental math, others containing numbers that might be better handled with paper and pencil.

Note that there will be no "right" way to sort the problems; a problem that seems easy to do mentally for one student may be beyond the capabilities of another. Encourage able mental calculators to explain to their classmates **how** they would do different problems in their heads.

Lesson 28   Adding Multiples of Ten

ABOUT THE LESSON

The problems presented in this lesson may be easy for many of your students, who should readily see their connection to the basic facts that they have already begun committing to memory. The instruction in this lesson is once again supported by physical models, for those who need the concrete experience.

An important goal of this lesson is to help students see that they do not need a written algorithm to do many arithmetic problems. They should begin to analyze problems before doing them and be able to choose the most efficient manner of attack (with either mental strategies or written algorithms).

YOU WILL NEED . . .
- Base ten blocks (longs and flats)
- Transparency 28, "Adding Tens"
- Power Builder 12, page 100

TEACHING THE LESSON

Place Transparency 28 on the overhead, covering all but the chart at the top. Lay out 3 longs (tens) in the space under "FIRST ADDEND." Name the amount represented (30) and write it in the strip below. To the right, lay out 4 longs. Name and write this number as well. (40) Now push all the longs together and ask students for the total. (70) If necessary, help the students count by tens to determine the answer. Record the total to complete the written problem.

Ask students what basic addition fact we could use to help us find the sum of 30 and 40. (3 + 4 = 7) As a clue, write on the board "3 tens + 4 tens = 7 tens."

Remind students that we could write this problem in vertical format and do it with a pencil, as we do with more difficult arithmetic problems. Ask, "Is this necessary? Why not?"

Next, display the problems in the middle of Transparency 28. Ask, "How are they alike?" (All involve multiples of ten, and as such are extensions of basic facts that can easily be done mentally.) You may want to model a few of these problems in the space above, using the base ten blocks. For extra practice, include several addition problems that contain three addends (such as 10 + 30 + 50) as well as some that

contain multiples of 100 (such as 300 + 400), which should be modeled using flats.

As a lesson wrap-up, work as a group through the TRY THESE problems at the bottom of the transparency, reminding students to add mentally. **ANSWERS: 1.** 80 **2.** 60 **3.** 60 **4.** 130 **5.** 100 **6.** 60 **7.** 120 **8.** 150 **9.** 120 **10.** 100

EXTENDING THE LESSON

Write on the board the problems listed below.

27 + 38	40 + 60
539 + 186	200 + 100 + 600
50 + 20 + 30	4,386 + 297

Ask students to tell which are easy to do mentally, which could be done mentally if enough time is given, and which are too difficult to do mentally. Have them explain their thinking in each case.

ORAL FOLLOW-UP

It is very important for students to practice mentally computing problems that are presented *orally* rather than visually. Read each of these problems aloud to students with *no* visual cues. Have them record only the answers, not the questions.

Fifty plus forty (90)
Seventy plus forty (110)
Three hundred plus eight hundred (1100)
Two hundred plus one hundred (300)
Thirty plus forty plus ten (80)
Twenty plus eighty plus fifty (150)
Forty plus ninety plus ten (140)
Five hundred plus one hundred plus three hundred (900)

You might ask students which method of presentation (oral or visual) they find easier. Research shows that people often use different techniques with different modes of presentation; some students prefer and are initially more successful with oral rather than visual presentation, while others prefer the visual approach.

INDIVIDUAL PRACTICE

Distribute copies of Power Builder 12 for additional practice or review of adding multiples of ten.

FIRST ADDEND   SECOND ADDEND

Write the problem here: ___ + ___ = ___

How are these alike?

40 + 60   70 + 20   30 + 50   30 + 10

TRY THESE IN YOUR HEAD.

1. 30 + 50	**3.** 50 + 10	**7.** 60 + 60
2. 40 + 20	**4.** 80 + 50	**8.** 70 + 80
	5. 70 + 30	**9.** 30 + 90
	6. 40 + 20	**10.** 80 + 20

Lesson 29   Adding a Multiple of Ten to a Number

ABOUT THE LESSON
This lesson is a natural extension of the preceding one; it also builds on lesson 25, in which the 100 chart was used as a model for adding tens to a number. In this lesson, students work through the same concept using base ten blocks.

YOU WILL NEED . . .
- Base ten blocks (units and longs; flats needed for extension only)
- Transparency 29, "Addition with Base Ten Blocks"
- Power Builder 13, page 101

TEACHING THE LESSON
Place Transparency 29 on the overhead, covering all but the chart at the top. Under the first heading, lay out 3 longs and 4 units. Ask students to name the number you have shown. (34)

Under the second heading add one long, then another, and another, each time asking students to name the entire number represented by the base ten blocks. (Starting with 34, students would then say "44, 54, 64.")

Write the expression 34 + 10 + 10 + 10 on the board and ask students for a "shorter" way to write it. (34 + 30) Record this in the appropriate space on the transparency. Ask students how the answer is like and different from the starting number. (The ones digit is the same; only the tens digit changed.)

Do several more of these counting sequences using base ten blocks on the transparency, each time beginning with a two-digit number and adding from 1 to 5 tens (initially keeping the answer less than 99). Be sure students see the written "short form" of the problem (such as 34 + 30) after each counting sequence so they can begin to go directly from this to the answer.

Display the center section of the transparency and ask for volunteers to represent the problems with base ten blocks. After doing these examples,

write 46 + 20 on the board. Ask students to describe how this problem might be modeled with the blocks. Then ask, "Can you add the numbers *mentally* (without using the base ten blocks)?" Encourage them to think, "46 plus 10 plus 10, or 46 . . . 56, 66."

Use the TRY THESE problems at the bottom of the transparency only as needed for additional guided practice. **ANSWERS: 1.** 52 **2.** 93 **3.** 56 **4.** 97 **5.** 86 **6.** 77 **7.** 115 **8.** 59 **9.** 65 **10.** 74

EXTENDING THE LESSON
Provide problems whose sum is more than 99. For example, model a problem such as 36 + 70 or 83 + 30 with base ten blocks. As 10 longs are collected, trade them for a flat (hundreds block). Encourage students to use the same "counting by tens" procedure that was highlighted in the lesson; that is, 83 + 30 is 83 + 10 + 10 + 10, or 83 . . . 93, 103, 113.

ORAL FOLLOW-UP
Ask students to listen to each of these problems as you read them slowly. Have them record only their final answers (not the problems themselves) on paper.

Thirty-four plus ten plus ten (54)
Fifty-two plus ten (62)
Sixteen plus ten plus ten plus ten plus ten (56)
Forty-eight plus ten plus ten plus ten plus ten plus ten (98)
Eighty-nine plus ten (99)
Sixty-four plus twenty (84)
Forty-nine plus forty (89)
Thirty-seven plus fifty (87)

INDIVIDUAL PRACTICE
Distribute copies of Power Builder 13 for additional practice or review of adding a multiple of ten to a number.

Show a number.

Then add . . .

Write the problem: ___ **+** ___ **=** ___

How would we
show these with
base ten blocks?

63 + 30

27 + 50

41 + 40

TRY THESE IN YOUR HEAD.

1.	32 + 20	**3.**	16 + 40	**7.**	45 + 70
2.	43 + 50	**4.**	67 + 30	**8.**	19 + 40
		5.	66 + 20	**9.**	55 + 10
		6.	27 + 50	**10.**	44 + 30

Lesson 30   Adding a Number Ending in 9

ABOUT THE LESSON
This lesson builds on the patterns established with the 100 chart in Unit Three. It focuses on a slightly more complicated mental math technique —adjusting an answer after adding a multiple of ten. For example, to add 19 to a number, we can add 20 and then subtract 1. You can use the 100 chart to reinforce how and why this technique works.

For many of your students, this technique will be a new one—one they have never used and probably never even heard of. Using this strategy represents a big step forward in mental math. It can be exciting for students to realize that we can use what we know about number patterns to simplify "messy looking" problems, making it possible to do them in our heads.

YOU WILL NEED . . .
• Transparency 30, "Making Problems Easier"
• Power Builder 14, page 102

TEACHING THE LESSON
Place Transparency 30 on the overhead and direct attention to the four problems at the top. Ask students what these problems have in common. (One addend of each problem ends in 9.) Ask if these problems would be "easy" to do in your head. Many students will likely answer no. Explain that you are going to show them a technique—a special trick—that will make these "messy" problems easier to do.

Begin with the problem 27 + 49, and have students compare it with 27 + 50. Ask, "How are the problems alike? How will the answers be different?" Lead them to see that 27 + 50 is just one more than 27 + 49. Ask, "Which problem is easier to add mentally, 27 + 50 or 27 + 49? Do you think we can use the answer to 27 + 50 to answer 27 + 49? How?"

Use the 100 chart to model 27 + 50: Start at 27, go down 5 rows, answer is 77. So, 27 + 49

must be one less, or 76. We could write the problem this way: 27 + 49 = 27 + 50 − 1.

Follow this technique as you go through each problem at the top of the transparency, doing 33 + 9 next. For each example, ask, "What easier problem can be helpful to us? How can we adjust the answer to this easier problem to find the answer to the given problem? How can we show this adjustment on the 100 chart?"

A similar technique can be used to mentally add problems in which one addend ends in 1, such as 37 + 11, 48 + 31, or 51 + 28. For example, to add 37 + 11, start with 37, add 10, then add 1. Adding numbers ending in 1 will likely be easier for students to do than adding numbers ending in 9. Because it can help them better understand the process of adjusting an answer, you may want to introduce the idea specifically for that purpose.

EXTENDING THE LESSON
Ask how we might use this technique to mentally add problems in which one addend ends in an 8. For example, to add 27 + 38, we could think, "That's the same as 27 + 40 − 2." Be sure to model this process on the 100 chart.

ORAL FOLLOW-UP
For those students who have a good mental picture of the 100 chart, encourage them to use it to mentally compute the following problems as you present them orally, rather then visually.

Fifty-nine plus twenty-seven (86)
Thirty-four plus thirty-nine (73)
Seventy-nine plus thirteen (92)
Sixty-seven plus nineteen (86)
Twenty-three plus forty-nine (72)
Seventy-eight plus nine (87)

INDIVIDUAL PRACTICE
Distribute copies of Power Builder 14 for additional practice or review of adding a number ending in 9.

Lesson 31   Adding by Expanding the Second Addend

ABOUT THE LESSON
This lesson features a way to make a "messy" (seemingly complicated) addition problem simpler—by expanding one of the addends. Be sure to emphasize the fact that for mental math, we always want to look for a shortcut method, one that will simplify the problem.

YOU WILL NEED ...
• Transparency 31, "Break It Up to Make It Easier"
• Power Builder 15, page 103

TEACHING THE LESSON
Begin the lesson by having students expand several two-digit numbers; for example, 43 is 40 + 3, 86 is 80 + 6, 37 is 30 + 7, and so forth.

Lead them to discover how this process can be helpful in mental addition. Write 25 + 43 on the board and ask if there is another way we could write this problem by expanding the 43. Write 25 + 40 + 3 on the board directly under 25 + 43. Call on a student to do this addition step by step and to explain why adding each step is easier than doing 25 + 43 all at once. (It's easy to add multiples of 10—like 40—in your head, and easy to add one-digit numbers to any other number.)

Place Transparency 31 on the overhead, covering all but the top section. Read it with the students; then uncover the next section and relate the mental math technique to carrying something heavy or doing anything difficult—it is always easier to take it one small part at a time. Using the transparency display, review how this technique works in the problem 25 + 43.

Display the three examples in the next section of the transparency and have students use the new technique to find the answers. You might record their work on the board, something like this:

PROBLEM   EXPANDED   STEP-BY-STEP SUM

24 + 35   24 + 30 + 5   24 + 30 + 5
                            54 + 5
                             59

Remind students that either (or both) of the addends could be expanded—whatever makes

the problem easiest. For example, we *could* think of 25 + 43 as 20 + 5 + 43 and add the addends in any order we choose. Or, we could expand both addends to get 20 + 5 + 40 + 3, and again add them in any order.

Use the TRY THESE problems at the bottom of the transparency for additional guided practice as needed. **ANSWERS: 1.** 41 **2.** 79 **3.** 98 **4.** 89 **5.** 98 **6.** 52 **7.** 69 **8.** 61 **9.** 84 **10.** 80

EXTENDING THE LESSON
The technique presented in this lesson could be extended to addition problems that contain more than two addends. For example:

   25 + 34 + 62 = 25 + 30 + 4 + 60 + 2

Although this *looks* more complicated, each step is simple. Give students the following problems and ask them to mentally compute the sum of each by expanding the last two addends:

   23 + 27 + 34   (84)
   45 + 16 + 23   (84)
   51 + 13 + 32   (96)
   67 + 12 + 21   (100)

ORAL FOLLOW-UP
Adding by expanding one of the addends is a bit more difficult if problems are presented orally, so you will need to modify your oral presentation.

The following examples (featuring problems with one addend already expanded) make a good oral practice set that can help students apply this new technique. Read each problem slowly, and ask students to write the final sum only.

   Twenty-seven plus twenty plus five (52)
   Forty-three plus ten plus six (59)
   Thirty-nine plus forty plus three (82)
   Forty-six plus twenty plus seven (73)
   Eighty-three plus ten plus five (98)
   Fifty-two plus twenty plus six (78)

INDIVIDUAL PRACTICE
Distribute copies of Power Builder 15 for additional practice or review of adding by expanding the second addend.

Is it too heavy to carry?
Break it up into smaller parts.

Does it look too hard to add in your head?
Break it up into smaller parts. Here's how:

25 + 43

25 + 40 + 3
65 + 3
68

How would you break up
these problems to make
them easier?

24 + 35

36 + 27

42 + 16

TRY THESE IN YOUR HEAD.

1. 27 + 14   **3.** 83 + 15   **7.** 27 + 42

2. 56 + 23   **4.** 56 + 33   **8.** 45 + 16

5. 73 + 25   **9.** 45 + 39

6. 34 + 18   **10.** 56 + 24

Lesson 32   Adding from the Front End

ABOUT THE LESSON
The technique presented in this lesson is a variation of adding by expanding (as presented in lesson 31). This new strategy—adding from the front end—reverses the steps of the written algorithm we teach for addition. Through this kind of experience, students begin to see computation as something flexible, an area in which *they* are in control of the skills to be used. This realization is an enormous step toward confidence and competence in mathematics.

YOU WILL NEED . . .
- Base ten blocks (units and longs)
- Transparency 32, "Adding from the Front End"
- Power Builder 16, page 104

TEACHING THE LESSON
Place Transparency 32 on the overhead, covering all but the top section. Focus attention on the problem 23 + 18. Model it in the space provided, using base ten blocks:

Point out that to add 23 and 18, we can join the tens (3 tens) and the ones (11 ones), and rename the sum (30 + 11 = 41). Remind students that when we add 23 and 18 using paper and pencil, we usually begin with the digits at the back end—the ones column (demonstrate as needed).

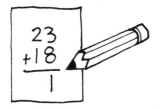

However, when working in our heads, it is often easier to begin with the front-end digits, in this case the tens, just as we did with the base ten blocks. This way, we are dealing with the most significant digits first—and it is natural to take care of the "big pieces" first. (You might remind students that they also work from left to right in reading.)

Display the three problems in the next section of the transparency and model them using the base ten blocks. As you proceed, demonstrate joining the tens first, then the ones, then finally the tens and ones together (for example, 45 + 39 = 7 tens and 14 ones, or 84).

As you work through the transparency, you might ask students to record the steps to each problem—writing the interim problem as was done with the first example—before asking them to do entire problems mentally.

This same procedure can be carried on into the TRY THESE guided practice problems as needed. **ANSWERS: 1.** 59 **2.** 80 **3.** 79 **4.** 86 **5.** 79 **6.** 61 **7.** 46 **8.** 63 **9.** 91 **10.** 93

EXTENDING THE LESSON
For more advanced students, try this front-end technique with problems involving three addends (23 + 49 + 16 = 7 tens and 18 ones, or 88) or with three-digit plus two-digit problems (184 + 27 = 20 tens and 11 ones, or 211).

ORAL FOLLOW-UP
The technique of adding from the front end does not lend itself well to problems given orally. However, an oral practice set like the one here can help prepare students to use the technique successfully. Ask students such questions on a regular basis.

What is 7 tens and 5 ones? (75)
What is 3 tens and 4 ones? (34)
What is 5 tens and 12 ones? (62)
What is 1 ten and 14 ones? (24)
What is 8 tens and 17 ones? (97)

INDIVIDUAL PRACTICE
Distribute copies of Power Builder 16 for additional practice or review of adding from the front end.

Show this problem using base ten blocks.

23 + 18

We can write this problem another way.

23 + 18 =

TENS	ONES		SUM
3	11	or	41

See how it works with these.

17 + 42

36 + 25

45 + 39

TRY THESE IN YOUR HEAD.

1. 43 + 16

2. 52 + 28

3. 56 + 23

4. 67 + 19

5. 33 + 46

6. 22 + 39

7. 28 + 18

8. 34 + 29

9. 77 + 14

10. 56 + 37

Lesson 33 Subtracting Multiples of Ten

ABOUT THE LESSON
This subtraction lesson parallels lesson 28, "Adding Multiples of Ten." It uses the same physical model, base ten blocks, to bridge from concrete experience to written algorithms to mental algorithms.

YOU WILL NEED . . .
- Base ten blocks (longs and flats)
- Transparency 33, "Subtracting Tens"
- Power Builder 17, page 105

TEACHING THE LESSON
Place Transparency 33 on the overhead, covering all but the chart at the top. Lay out 7 longs (tens) as the starting number. Ask students what number you have shown. (70) Then take away 3 longs, one at a time, moving them to the side. Each time you remove a long, ask students to name the number left. Thus, as you take away 3 longs, they will say "60 . . . 50 . . . 40."

Start over with 70 and take away 5 longs one by one, having students name the number left each time you remove another one. Continue this activity using different multiples of ten as starting numbers.

Now start again with 7 longs. (70) This time move 3 longs *as a single group* to the side. Ask, "What number have I taken away? (30) What number is left? (40)" Repeat this with several other numbers; for example, 70 take away 20, 70 take away 50, 50 take away 10, 90 take away 40, and so on. After doing a few, begin to show the written form of each problem in the space allotted on the transparency. Ask students to name a basic fact that is similar to each problem. For example, they should be able to relate 70 − 20 = 50 to the basic fact 7 − 2 = 5.

Uncover the problems in the next section of the transparency and ask students how they are different from the problems you have been doing with the base ten blocks. (These involve hundreds rather than tens.) Ask them to name a basic fact that is similar to each problem, then mentally subtract and give the answer. If necessary, use flats to model the problems. You might remind students of the written algorithm they generally use when doing more complex problems and ask why that approach is unnecessary for these problems.

Use the TRY THESE problems for additional practice as necessary. **ANSWERS: 1.** 40 **2.** 80 **3.** 50 **4.** 10 **5.** 40 **6.** 90 **7.** 300 **8.** 200 **9.** 500 **10.** 400

EXTENDING THE LESSON
You might extend this lesson by asking students to transfer what they've learned to problems involving multiples of a thousand or to problems that involve two or more subtrahends. For example:

4,000 − 3,000	8,000 − 1,000
9,000 − 2,000	12,000 − 7,000
90 − 30 − 40	150 − 70 − 30
800 − 200 − 100	1200 − 600 − 200

ORAL FOLLOW-UP
Give the following set of exercises orally a day or two following this lesson. Read each problem slowly.

Eighty take away thirty (50)

Ninety minus sixty (30)

Take thirty away from one hundred twenty (90)

One hundred sixty minus eighty (80)

Seven hundred minus two hundred (500)

Eight hundred less four hundred (400)

Fifteen hundred minus eight hundred (700)

Six hundred subtracted from fourteen hundred (800)

INDIVIDUAL PRACTICE
Distribute copies of Power Builder 17 for additional practice or review of subtracting multiples of ten.

Show a number.   Then take away . . .

Write the problem here: _____ − _____ = _____

Could you do these with base ten blocks?

$600 - 200$

$1100 - 300$

$500 - 400$

TRY THESE IN YOUR HEAD.

1. 70 − 30   **3.** 90 − 40   **7.** 500 − 200

2. 90 − 10   **4.** 70 − 60   **8.** 800 − 600

            5. 120 − 80   **9.** 1000 − 500

            6. 150 − 60   **10.** 1300 − 900

Lesson 34   Subtracting a Multiple of Ten from a Number

ABOUT THE LESSON
This lesson parallels lesson 29, "Adding a Multiple of Ten to a Number." It uses the same model, base ten blocks. You may also want to refer to the 100 chart model while developing this lesson. Some students find it as helpful as base ten blocks and may benefit from having a second visual model.

YOU WILL NEED . . .
• Base ten blocks (units and longs)
• Transparency 34, "Subtraction with Base Ten Blocks"
• Power Builder 18, page 106

TEACHING THE LESSON
Place Transparency 34 on the overhead, covering all but the top section. Lay 6 longs (tens) and 3 units (ones) under the first heading. Ask students to name the number you have shown. (63) Explain that you are going to be taking away some blocks, but only the longs. Begin taking away one long at a time, moving them to the right. Each time you take away one long, ask students to name the number left.

After you've removed 2 longs, write the expression $63 - 10 - 10$ on the board. Also write the number represented. (43) Ask students how this number is like and how it is different from 63. (It has the same number of ones and a different number of tens.) Ask students what we have taken away altogether. (20) Ask if anyone can think of a shorter way to write the problem. ($63 - 20 = 43$) Record this in the space for the written problem on the transparency.

Repeat this activity several times with other problems, using base ten blocks and the transparency. For example:

$63 - 10 - 10 - 10 - 10$, or $63 - 40$
$71 - 10 - 10 - 10$, or $71 - 30$
$57 - 10 - 10 - 10 - 10 - 10$, or $57 - 50$

Emphasize both the counting-down sequences and the final written form of the problem so that students can eventually go directly from the written form to the answer.

Use the TRY THESE problems as needed to provide additional guided practice. **ANSWERS: 1.** 25 **2.** 48 **3.** 46 **4.** 38 **5.** 41 **6.** 37 **7.** 45 **8.** 24 **9.** 14 **10.** 29

EXTENDING THE LESSON
Provide problems with a minuend greater than 99 and a subtrahend that is a multiple of 10, such as $123 - 20$, $146 - 30$, and $153 - 60$. Point out that the answer will, in each case, have the same number of ones as the minuend. See if students can explain why. Help students focus on mentally subtracting the tens. For example, in **123 - 20**, 12 tens minus 2 tens is 10 tens or 100, so the answer is 103.

ORAL FOLLOW-UP
A day or two after this lesson, read the problems below and ask students to do them in their heads. Read each problem slowly and repeat as necessary.

Fifty-six minus twenty (36)
Eighty-three minus thirty (53)
Ninety-one minus seventy (21)
Forty-six minus forty (6)
Eighty-one minus thirty (51)
Fifty-nine minus forty (19)
Forty-eight minus twenty (28)
Ninety-nine minus seventy (29)

INDIVIDUAL PRACTICE
Distribute copies of Power Builder 18 for additional practice or review of subtracting a multiple of ten from a number.

Show a number.

Then take away . . .

Write the problem:

TRY THESE IN YOUR HEAD.

1. 45 − 20

2. 78 − 30

3. 56 − 10

4. 88 − 50

5. 71 − 30

6. 87 − 50

7. 85 − 40

8. 94 − 70

9. 94 − 80

10. 99 − 70

Lesson 35　Subtracting a Number Ending in 9

ABOUT THE LESSON

This lesson parallels lesson 30, "Adding a Number Ending in 9." However, most students will find the adjusting technique a bit more difficult to apply to subtraction.

You will probably want to review the technique for adding a number ending in 9 (add the next higher number, then subtract one) before introducing the technique for subtracting a number ending in 9 (subtract the next higher number, then *add* one). Setting it up in parallel this way can help students see why the adjusting step involves *adding* one, even though the original problem involves subtraction.

YOU WILL NEED . . .

- Transparency 30, "Making Problems Easier" (optional, for review)
- Transparency 35, "Making Subtraction Problems Easier"
- The 100 Chart (page 115, or bulletin board display)
- Power Builder 19, page 107

TEACHING THE LESSON

With or without Transparency 30 on the overhead, review with students the strategy introduced in lesson 30 for mentally adding problems such as 27 + 49; that is, think of the problem as 27 + 50 – 1. Briefly discuss how changing one of the numbers in the problem to another form—that is, changing 49 to (50 – 1) —made the problem easier to do even though it added a step.

Next place Transparency 35 on the overhead and cover all but the section at the top. Ask students to identify how these four problems are alike. Then have them compare these problems to the ones shown in lesson 30. How are they alike? How are they different?

Demonstrate the adjusting technique for subtraction using the problem 47 – 19. Explain the process in words as you display the written form in the middle of the transparency. Say:

> Start with 47. Nineteen is close to 20, so subtract 20 . . . that's 27. But we subtracted 1 too many, so add 1 . . . that's 28.

Some students will find the verbal explanation more helpful than the written equation. Be sure to

have students talk out their thinking processes as they mentally compute. This verbalization will help them solidify the technique in their own thinking.

Continue to work through the problems at the top of the transparency. Demonstrate the adjusting technique for each one. Then use the 100 chart to visually model the process. For example, for 51 – 29, start at 51 on the chart. Subtract 30 (go up 3 blocks), then add 1 (go to the right 1 block) to arrive at 22.

At this stage, students may be able to apply the strategy themselves, but may need a model (the 100 chart) or the written form to work through a problem. Don't discourage this use of an intermediate support. As students become more confident and proficient, you can encourage them to do the work entirely in their heads.

Use the TRY THESE problems for additional practice and discussion. **ANSWERS: 1.** 44 **2.** 57 **3.** 48 **4.** 16 **5.** 27 **6.** 15 **7.** 54 **8.** 49 **9.** 45 **10.** 12

EXTENDING THE LESSON

Ask students how the adjusting strategy developed in this lesson can be applied to the problem 43 – 18. (We can think of it as 43 – 20 + 2.) Talk through this extension of the technique, using the 100 chart as necessary. Give practice with problems like the following:

37 – 8	(37 – 10 + 2 = 29)
53 – 28	(53 – 30 + 2 = 25)
42 – 18	(42 – 20 + 2 = 24)
65 – 38	(65 – 40 + 2 = 27)
39 – 18	(39 – 20 + 2 = 21)
94 – 48	(94 – 50 + 2 = 46)

ORAL FOLLOW-UP

Orally present problems with the adjusting step already done. For example:

Forty-one minus ten plus one (32)
Thirty-eight minus ten plus one (29)
Eighty-four minus twenty plus one (65)

INDIVIDUAL PRACTICE

Distribute copies of Power Builder 19 for additional practice or review of subtracting a number ending in 9.

47 − 19   35 − 9

51 − 29   96 − 49

How are these problems alike?

Can you think of an easy way
to do them in your head?

47 − 19

Think:

$$47 - 19 = 47 - 20 + 1$$
$$= 27 + 1$$
$$= 28$$

TRY THESE IN YOUR HEAD.

1. 53 − 9   **3.** 67 − 19   **7.** 83 − 29

2. 66 − 9   **4.** 45 − 29   **8.** 88 − 39

                5. 76 − 49   **9.** 64 − 19

                6. 44 − 29   **10.** 61 − 49

ABOUT THE LESSON
This lesson focuses on subtraction problems in which both numbers have the same units digit, such as 45 – 15 or 57 – 37. Your students will likely find this a simple lesson. Even so, be careful not to rush through the development or to assume too much of the students.

Along with other lessons in this unit, this one helps students learn to discriminate between problems that can be done easily in the head and those that are better suited to a written method.

YOU WILL NEED . . .
• Transparency 36, "Easy Endings"
• Base ten blocks (units and longs)
• Power Builder 20, page 108

TEACHING THE LESSON
Place Transparency 36 on the overhead and cover all but the four problems and chart at the top. Use base ten blocks to represent the problem 64 – 24; that is, lay out 6 longs (tens) and 4 units (ones), then take away 2 tens and 4 ones, leaving an answer of 4 tens, or 40. Ask student volunteers to use the base ten blocks to demonstrate the other problems above the chart.

Ask, "What is alike about each of the problems? (The two numbers in each problem contain the same units digit.) What's alike about each answer? (All end in 0.)"

On the board, set up these same four problems using the written algorithm:

```
  64        47        58        73
 -24       -17       -28       -53
```

Explain that if we were working with paper and pencil, we would begin with the ones digit in each case. Point out that no regrouping is necessary when the ending digits are the same. When no regrouping is necessary, we can do problems such as these *without* writing them and

without using the traditional algorithm. They're easy to do in our heads.

Now display the six problems in the next section of the transparency. Ask students to choose all the problems that fit the pattern we have just described. After identifying them, students should mentally compute the answers.

Use the TRY THESE problems for additional guided practice as needed. **ANSWERS: 1.** 40 **2.** 20 **3.** 10 **4.** 50 **5.** 10 **6.** 40 **7.** 50 **8.** 10 **9.** 40 **10.** 90

EXTENDING THE LESSON
This lesson has focused on problems with *like* endings (same ones digit), in which the subtraction is easy to do mentally because no regrouping is involved. You might extend this lesson by providing problems that require no regrouping but do *not* contain like endings. Such problems are similarly easy to figure mentally. For example:

28 – 14	(14)	87 – 34	(53)
37 – 25	(12)	63 – 22	(41)
83 – 12	(71)	56 – 45	(11)
58 – 43	(15)	99 – 14	(85)

ORAL FOLLOW-UP
Present the following problems orally:
Twenty-eight minus eight (20)
Forty-six minus twenty-six (20)
Sixty-three minus fifty-three (10)
Seventy-two minus thirty-two (40)
Ninety-seven minus forty-seven (50)
Twenty-five minus fifteen (10)
Seventy-one minus eleven (60)
Eighty-eight minus seventy-eight (10)

INDIVIDUAL PRACTICE
Distribute copies of Power Builder 20 for additional practice or review of subtracting numbers with like endings.

Use base ten blocks to show these problems.

| 64 – 24 | 47 – 17 | 58 – 28 | 73 – 53 |

Show a number.   Then take away . . .

Which of these
problems fit the
same pattern?

| 40 – 27 | 53 – 33 | 96 – 48 |

| 38 – 25 | 46 – 16 | 79 – 39 |

TRY THESE IN YOUR HEAD.

1. 89 – 49   **3.** 56 – 46   **7.** 78 – 28

2. 77 – 57   **4.** 88 – 38   **8.** 29 – 19

                   5. 59 – 49   **9.** 57 – 17

                   6. 47 – 7   **10.** 93 – 3

Unit Four Progress Test

The fifteen-item test below, intended for timed oral presentation, is designed to measure students' mental computation skills in the concepts presented in Unit Four.

Have the students write their names at the top of a sheet of lined paper and number from 1 to 15. Instruct them to write the answer to each problem after the proper number. Emphasize that they will have only 5 seconds to compute the answer in their heads and write it before you go on to the next problem.

Read the problem number, then the problem. Repeat it, wait 5 to 7 seconds, then read the next question.

UNIT FOUR TEST	ANSWERS
1. What is 60 and 20?	**1.** 80
2. 40 plus 30	**2.** 70
3. What is 30 less than 90?	**3.** 60
4. What is 50 more than 17?	**4.** 67
5. 96 minus 70	**5.** 26
6. What is 30 less than 78?	**6.** 48
7. 27 plus 49	**7.** 76
8. 32 plus 39	**8.** 71
9. What is 43 more than 25?	**9.** 68
10. 65 plus 26	**10.** 91
11. 18 plus 74	**11.** 92
12. 53 minus 29	**12.** 24
13. 86 minus 69	**13.** 17
14. 95 take away 45	**14.** 50
15. 73 minus 43	**15.** 30

Counting On

1.
$$\begin{array}{r}7\\+2\\\hline\end{array}\quad\begin{array}{r}5\\+3\\\hline\end{array}\quad\begin{array}{r}8\\+1\\\hline\end{array}\quad\begin{array}{r}4\\+2\\\hline\end{array}\quad\begin{array}{r}8\\+3\\\hline\end{array}\quad\begin{array}{r}9\\+1\\\hline\end{array}\quad\begin{array}{r}3\\+6\\\hline\end{array}\quad\begin{array}{r}2\\+5\\\hline\end{array}$$

2.
$$\begin{array}{r}3\\+7\\\hline\end{array}\quad\begin{array}{r}4\\+1\\\hline\end{array}\quad\begin{array}{r}6\\+2\\\hline\end{array}\quad\begin{array}{r}2\\+9\\\hline\end{array}\quad\begin{array}{r}1\\+5\\\hline\end{array}\quad\begin{array}{r}3\\+4\\\hline\end{array}\quad\begin{array}{r}6\\+1\\\hline\end{array}\quad\begin{array}{r}8\\+2\\\hline\end{array}$$

3.
$$\begin{array}{r}2\\+4\\\hline\end{array}\quad\begin{array}{r}7\\+1\\\hline\end{array}\quad\begin{array}{r}5\\+2\\\hline\end{array}\quad\begin{array}{r}1\\+8\\\hline\end{array}\quad\begin{array}{r}9\\+3\\\hline\end{array}\quad\begin{array}{r}6\\+3\\\hline\end{array}\quad\begin{array}{r}3\\+8\\\hline\end{array}\quad\begin{array}{r}1\\+9\\\hline\end{array}$$

4.
$$\begin{array}{r}2\\+7\\\hline\end{array}\quad\begin{array}{r}3\\+9\\\hline\end{array}\quad\begin{array}{r}4\\+3\\\hline\end{array}\quad\begin{array}{r}2\\+8\\\hline\end{array}\quad\begin{array}{r}3\\+5\\\hline\end{array}\quad\begin{array}{r}7\\+3\\\hline\end{array}\quad\begin{array}{r}9\\+2\\\hline\end{array}\quad\begin{array}{r}5\\+1\\\hline\end{array}$$

Using Doubles

1.　6　　8　　5　　9　　4　　6　　6　　8
　　　+6　+7　+6　+7　+4　+8　+4　+9

2.　4　　6　　9　　3　　7　　5　　9　　3
　　　+5　+7　+8　+4　+7　+7　+9　+3

3.　7　　8　　7　　7　　6　　8　　4　　9
　　　+8　+9　+5　+9　+6　+6　+6　+8

4.　4　　5　　7　　3　　5　　8　　3　　5
　　　+3　+5　+6　+3　+7　+8　+5　+4

Making Ten and Adding with Ten

1.
$\begin{array}{r} 4 \\ +6 \\ \hline \end{array}$
$\begin{array}{r} 10 \\ +3 \\ \hline \end{array}$
$\begin{array}{r} 9 \\ +5 \\ \hline \end{array}$
$\begin{array}{r} 6 \\ +10 \\ \hline \end{array}$
$\begin{array}{r} 7 \\ +3 \\ \hline \end{array}$
$\begin{array}{r} 8 \\ +5 \\ \hline \end{array}$
$\begin{array}{r} 4 \\ +9 \\ \hline \end{array}$
$\begin{array}{r} 2 \\ +8 \\ \hline \end{array}$

2.
$\begin{array}{r} 9 \\ +6 \\ \hline \end{array}$
$\begin{array}{r} 1 \\ +9 \\ \hline \end{array}$
$\begin{array}{r} 8 \\ +4 \\ \hline \end{array}$
$\begin{array}{r} 10 \\ +5 \\ \hline \end{array}$
$\begin{array}{r} 6 \\ +4 \\ \hline \end{array}$
$\begin{array}{r} 2 \\ +10 \\ \hline \end{array}$
$\begin{array}{r} 3 \\ +8 \\ \hline \end{array}$
$\begin{array}{r} 10 \\ +4 \\ \hline \end{array}$

3.
$\begin{array}{r} 3 \\ +7 \\ \hline \end{array}$
$\begin{array}{r} 5 \\ +8 \\ \hline \end{array}$
$\begin{array}{r} 7 \\ +10 \\ \hline \end{array}$
$\begin{array}{r} 5 \\ +9 \\ \hline \end{array}$
$\begin{array}{r} 8 \\ +2 \\ \hline \end{array}$
$\begin{array}{r} 10 \\ +6 \\ \hline \end{array}$
$\begin{array}{r} 9 \\ +4 \\ \hline \end{array}$
$\begin{array}{r} 10 \\ +3 \\ \hline \end{array}$

4.
$\begin{array}{r} 10 \\ +2 \\ \hline \end{array}$
$\begin{array}{r} 9 \\ +3 \\ \hline \end{array}$
$\begin{array}{r} 8 \\ +3 \\ \hline \end{array}$
$\begin{array}{r} 5 \\ +10 \\ \hline \end{array}$
$\begin{array}{r} 4 \\ +8 \\ \hline \end{array}$
$\begin{array}{r} 5 \\ +5 \\ \hline \end{array}$
$\begin{array}{r} 3 \\ +9 \\ \hline \end{array}$
$\begin{array}{r} 9 \\ +1 \\ \hline \end{array}$

Basic Facts in Addition

1.
$$\begin{array}{r} 8 \\ +5 \\ \hline \end{array} \quad \begin{array}{r} 9 \\ +6 \\ \hline \end{array} \quad \begin{array}{r} 2 \\ +1 \\ \hline \end{array} \quad \begin{array}{r} 3 \\ +6 \\ \hline \end{array} \quad \begin{array}{r} 3 \\ +3 \\ \hline \end{array} \quad \begin{array}{r} 8 \\ +9 \\ \hline \end{array} \quad \begin{array}{r} 2 \\ +4 \\ \hline \end{array} \quad \begin{array}{r} 3 \\ +4 \\ \hline \end{array}$$

2.
$$\begin{array}{r} 2 \\ +8 \\ \hline \end{array} \quad \begin{array}{r} 3 \\ +1 \\ \hline \end{array} \quad \begin{array}{r} 7 \\ +9 \\ \hline \end{array} \quad \begin{array}{r} 8 \\ +3 \\ \hline \end{array} \quad \begin{array}{r} 2 \\ +6 \\ \hline \end{array} \quad \begin{array}{r} 9 \\ +9 \\ \hline \end{array} \quad \begin{array}{r} 4 \\ +9 \\ \hline \end{array} \quad \begin{array}{r} 2 \\ +9 \\ \hline \end{array}$$

3.
$$\begin{array}{r} 6 \\ +3 \\ \hline \end{array} \quad \begin{array}{r} 8 \\ +6 \\ \hline \end{array} \quad \begin{array}{r} 8 \\ +4 \\ \hline \end{array} \quad \begin{array}{r} 6 \\ +8 \\ \hline \end{array} \quad \begin{array}{r} 1 \\ +2 \\ \hline \end{array} \quad \begin{array}{r} 1 \\ +6 \\ \hline \end{array} \quad \begin{array}{r} 5 \\ +9 \\ \hline \end{array} \quad \begin{array}{r} 6 \\ +5 \\ \hline \end{array}$$

4.
$$\begin{array}{r} 2 \\ +2 \\ \hline \end{array} \quad \begin{array}{r} 8 \\ +2 \\ \hline \end{array} \quad \begin{array}{r} 9 \\ +4 \\ \hline \end{array} \quad \begin{array}{r} 1 \\ +3 \\ \hline \end{array} \quad \begin{array}{r} 4 \\ +5 \\ \hline \end{array} \quad \begin{array}{r} 4 \\ +7 \\ \hline \end{array} \quad \begin{array}{r} 5 \\ +2 \\ \hline \end{array} \quad \begin{array}{r} 3 \\ +7 \\ \hline \end{array}$$

5.
$$\begin{array}{r} 4 \\ +3 \\ \hline \end{array} \quad \begin{array}{r} 5 \\ +7 \\ \hline \end{array} \quad \begin{array}{r} 7 \\ +1 \\ \hline \end{array} \quad \begin{array}{r} 1 \\ +9 \\ \hline \end{array} \quad \begin{array}{r} 2 \\ +5 \\ \hline \end{array} \quad \begin{array}{r} 3 \\ +8 \\ \hline \end{array} \quad \begin{array}{r} 5 \\ +6 \\ \hline \end{array} \quad \begin{array}{r} 1 \\ +5 \\ \hline \end{array}$$

Basic Facts in Addition

1.
$$
\begin{array}{cccccccc}
6 & 1 & 8 & 6 & 6 & 4 & 5 & 8 \\
+9 & +7 & +1 & +7 & +2 & +2 & +3 & +8 \\
\end{array}
$$

2.
$$
\begin{array}{cccccccc}
9 & 6 & 8 & 1 & 9 & 2 & 3 & 7 \\
+2 & +1 & +7 & +4 & +3 & +7 & +2 & +8 \\
\end{array}
$$

3.
$$
\begin{array}{cccccccc}
7 & 4 & 5 & 3 & 2 & 5 & 7 & 7 \\
+3 & +4 & +1 & +5 & +3 & +5 & +2 & +5 \\
\end{array}
$$

4.
$$
\begin{array}{cccccccc}
7 & 6 & 7 & 3 & 5 & 1 & 7 & 6 \\
+4 & +6 & +7 & +9 & +8 & +8 & +6 & +4 \\
\end{array}
$$

5.
$$
\begin{array}{cccccccc}
9 & 5 & 4 & 4 & 9 & 9 & 4 & 9 \\
+1 & +4 & +8 & +1 & +7 & +8 & +6 & +5 \\
\end{array}
$$

Counting Back

1. $\begin{array}{r} 9 \\ -2 \\ \hline \end{array}$ $\begin{array}{r} 7 \\ -3 \\ \hline \end{array}$ $\begin{array}{r} 4 \\ -1 \\ \hline \end{array}$ $\begin{array}{r} 6 \\ -1 \\ \hline \end{array}$ $\begin{array}{r} 10 \\ -1 \\ \hline \end{array}$ $\begin{array}{r} 5 \\ -2 \\ \hline \end{array}$ $\begin{array}{r} 11 \\ -3 \\ \hline \end{array}$ $\begin{array}{r} 3 \\ -1 \\ \hline \end{array}$

2. $\begin{array}{r} 5 \\ -3 \\ \hline \end{array}$ $\begin{array}{r} 9 \\ -1 \\ \hline \end{array}$ $\begin{array}{r} 7 \\ -2 \\ \hline \end{array}$ $\begin{array}{r} 3 \\ -2 \\ \hline \end{array}$ $\begin{array}{r} 6 \\ -3 \\ \hline \end{array}$ $\begin{array}{r} 8 \\ -2 \\ \hline \end{array}$ $\begin{array}{r} 5 \\ -1 \\ \hline \end{array}$ $\begin{array}{r} 4 \\ -2 \\ \hline \end{array}$

3. $\begin{array}{r} 4 \\ -2 \\ \hline \end{array}$ $\begin{array}{r} 8 \\ -3 \\ \hline \end{array}$ $\begin{array}{r} 7 \\ -1 \\ \hline \end{array}$ $\begin{array}{r} 12 \\ -3 \\ \hline \end{array}$ $\begin{array}{r} 8 \\ -1 \\ \hline \end{array}$ $\begin{array}{r} 11 \\ -3 \\ \hline \end{array}$ $\begin{array}{r} 9 \\ -3 \\ \hline \end{array}$ $\begin{array}{r} 10 \\ -2 \\ \hline \end{array}$

4. $\begin{array}{r} 11 \\ -2 \\ \hline \end{array}$ $\begin{array}{r} 4 \\ -3 \\ \hline \end{array}$ $\begin{array}{r} 6 \\ -2 \\ \hline \end{array}$ $\begin{array}{r} 10 \\ -3 \\ \hline \end{array}$ $\begin{array}{r} 3 \\ -1 \\ \hline \end{array}$ $\begin{array}{r} 12 \\ -3 \\ \hline \end{array}$ $\begin{array}{r} 10 \\ -2 \\ \hline \end{array}$ $\begin{array}{r} 6 \\ -1 \\ \hline \end{array}$

Counting Up

1.
6	9	12	7	9	8	4	5
−4	−8	−9	−5	−6	−7	−3	−3

2.
5	6	10	8	11	4	8	10
−4	−6	−8	−5	−8	−4	−6	−7

3.
9	8	10	7	6	12	10	5
−7	−8	−9	−4	−5	−9	−8	−4

4.
11	9	10	8	7	11	5	12
−9	−6	−7	−5	−6	−8	−3	−9

Thinking Addition

1.
12	14	11	16	15	10	13	9
−7	−6	−5	−8	−7	−3	−6	−5

2.
16	17	14	10	12	11	8	12
−7	−8	−7	−4	−5	−4	−3	−4

3.
13	14	18	15	15	9	16	11
−5	−8	−9	−8	−6	−4	−9	−3

4.
11	14	13	10	14	17	13	10
−6	−9	−7	−6	−5	−9	−8	−7

Using "Make Ten" Combinations

1.
$$\begin{array}{cccccccc} 13 & 15 & 17 & 13 & 14 & 12 & 15 & 12 \\ \underline{-9} & \underline{-8} & \underline{-9} & \underline{-7} & \underline{-8} & \underline{-9} & \underline{-7} & \underline{-8} \end{array}$$

2.
$$\begin{array}{cccccccc} 13 & 15 & 12 & 16 & 14 & 11 & 10 & 18 \\ \underline{-8} & \underline{-9} & \underline{-7} & \underline{-9} & \underline{-7} & \underline{-8} & \underline{-7} & \underline{-9} \end{array}$$

3.
$$\begin{array}{cccccccc} 16 & 12 & 14 & 17 & 11 & 16 & 12 & 14 \\ \underline{-8} & \underline{-8} & \underline{-9} & \underline{-9} & \underline{-7} & \underline{-7} & \underline{-9} & \underline{-8} \end{array}$$

4.
$$\begin{array}{cccccccc} 16 & 18 & 11 & 15 & 17 & 16 & 14 & 16 \\ \underline{-8} & \underline{-9} & \underline{-9} & \underline{-9} & \underline{-8} & \underline{-7} & \underline{-6} & \underline{-9} \end{array}$$

Basic Facts in Subtraction

1.
$$\begin{array}{cccccccc} 6 & 7 & 8 & 9 & 13 & 7 & 15 & 14 \\ -5 & -6 & -7 & -2 & -5 & -4 & -7 & -7 \end{array}$$

2.
$$\begin{array}{cccccccc} 12 & 10 & 3 & 14 & 14 & 4 & 10 & 12 \\ -4 & -6 & -1 & -8 & -6 & -2 & -8 & -7 \end{array}$$

3.
$$\begin{array}{cccccccc} 9 & 16 & 10 & 13 & 8 & 9 & 12 & 10 \\ -6 & -7 & -4 & -4 & -1 & -4 & -3 & -2 \end{array}$$

4.
$$\begin{array}{cccccccc} 10 & 18 & 9 & 14 & 12 & 15 & 6 & 3 \\ -3 & -9 & -1 & -9 & -8 & -9 & -4 & -2 \end{array}$$

5.
$$\begin{array}{cccccccc} 15 & 10 & 11 & 8 & 17 & 11 & 9 & 11 \\ -8 & -5 & -3 & -5 & -9 & -2 & -3 & -6 \end{array}$$

Basic Facts in Subtraction

1. $\begin{array}{r} 8 \\ -3 \\ \hline \end{array}$ $\begin{array}{r} 4 \\ -1 \\ \hline \end{array}$ $\begin{array}{r} 5 \\ -1 \\ \hline \end{array}$ $\begin{array}{r} 9 \\ -8 \\ \hline \end{array}$ $\begin{array}{r} 6 \\ -2 \\ \hline \end{array}$ $\begin{array}{r} 6 \\ -1 \\ \hline \end{array}$ $\begin{array}{r} 12 \\ -9 \\ \hline \end{array}$ $\begin{array}{r} 7 \\ -2 \\ \hline \end{array}$

2. $\begin{array}{r} 4 \\ -3 \\ \hline \end{array}$ $\begin{array}{r} 11 \\ -7 \\ \hline \end{array}$ $\begin{array}{r} 5 \\ -4 \\ \hline \end{array}$ $\begin{array}{r} 9 \\ -5 \\ \hline \end{array}$ $\begin{array}{r} 12 \\ -6 \\ \hline \end{array}$ $\begin{array}{r} 11 \\ -4 \\ \hline \end{array}$ $\begin{array}{r} 13 \\ -6 \\ \hline \end{array}$ $\begin{array}{r} 8 \\ -2 \\ \hline \end{array}$

3. $\begin{array}{r} 10 \\ -7 \\ \hline \end{array}$ $\begin{array}{r} 16 \\ -8 \\ \hline \end{array}$ $\begin{array}{r} 13 \\ -8 \\ \hline \end{array}$ $\begin{array}{r} 10 \\ -1 \\ \hline \end{array}$ $\begin{array}{r} 14 \\ -5 \\ \hline \end{array}$ $\begin{array}{r} 7 \\ -3 \\ \hline \end{array}$ $\begin{array}{r} 11 \\ -9 \\ \hline \end{array}$ $\begin{array}{r} 13 \\ -7 \\ \hline \end{array}$

4. $\begin{array}{r} 5 \\ -2 \\ \hline \end{array}$ $\begin{array}{r} 17 \\ -8 \\ \hline \end{array}$ $\begin{array}{r} 9 \\ -7 \\ \hline \end{array}$ $\begin{array}{r} 5 \\ -3 \\ \hline \end{array}$ $\begin{array}{r} 12 \\ -5 \\ \hline \end{array}$ $\begin{array}{r} 11 \\ -5 \\ \hline \end{array}$ $\begin{array}{r} 7 \\ -1 \\ \hline \end{array}$ $\begin{array}{r} 6 \\ -3 \\ \hline \end{array}$

5. $\begin{array}{r} 15 \\ -6 \\ \hline \end{array}$ $\begin{array}{r} 8 \\ -4 \\ \hline \end{array}$ $\begin{array}{r} 8 \\ -6 \\ \hline \end{array}$ $\begin{array}{r} 13 \\ -9 \\ \hline \end{array}$ $\begin{array}{r} 11 \\ -8 \\ \hline \end{array}$ $\begin{array}{r} 7 \\ -5 \\ \hline \end{array}$ $\begin{array}{r} 16 \\ -9 \\ \hline \end{array}$ $\begin{array}{r} 10 \\ -9 \\ \hline \end{array}$

Adding Multiples of Ten

1. $40 + 50 =$ _____

2. $30 + 10 =$ _____

3. $20 + 70 =$ _____

4. $80 + 30 =$ _____

5. $40 + 60 =$ _____

6. $90 + 20 =$ _____

7. $50 + 50 =$ _____

8. $30 + 80 =$ _____

9. $10 + 70 =$ _____

10. $70 + 50 =$ _____

11. $90 + 50 =$ _____

12. $10 + 90 =$ _____

13. $40 + 20 =$ _____

14. $20 + 80 =$ _____

15. $90 + 40 =$ _____

16. $60 + 50 =$ _____

17. $30 + 20 + 10 =$ _____

18. $20 + 20 + 50 =$ _____

19. $50 + 40 + 20 =$ _____

20. $10 + 30 + 90 =$ _____

Adding a Multiple of Ten to a Number

1. 27 + 10 = _____

2. 43 + 10 = _____

3. 38 + 10 = _____

4. 74 + 10 = _____

5. 62 + 10 + 10 = _____

6. 17 + 10 + 10 = _____

7. 14 + 10 + 10 = _____

8. 38 + 10 + 10 + 10 = _____

9. 43 + 10 + 10 + 10 = _____

10. 26 + 10 + 10 = _____

11. 36 + 20 = _____

12. 73 + 20 = _____

13. 84 + 10 = _____

14. 51 + 30 = _____

15. 57 + 20 = _____

16. 45 + 40 = _____

17. 52 + 40 = _____

18. 62 + 10 = _____

19. 13 + 40 = _____

20. 18 + 50 = _____

Adding a Number Ending in 9

1. $34 + 9 =$ _____

2. $82 + 9 =$ _____

3. $15 + 9 =$ _____

4. $23 + 9 =$ _____

5. $26 + 9 =$ _____

6. $43 + 9 =$ _____

7. $38 + 19 =$ _____

8. $52 + 19 =$ _____

9. $65 + 19 =$ _____

10. $74 + 19 =$ _____

11. $38 + 29 =$ _____

12. $43 + 39 =$ _____

13. $52 + 29 =$ _____

14. $26 + 29 =$ _____

15. $19 + 49 =$ _____

16. $38 + 39 =$ _____

17. $51 + 39 =$ _____

18. $62 + 19 =$ _____

19. $82 + 19 =$ _____

20. $43 + 29 =$ _____

Adding by Expanding the Second Addend

1. $53 + 30 =$ _____

2. $53 + 30 + 2 =$ _____

3. $84 + 10 =$ _____

4. $84 + 10 + 7 =$ _____

5. $43 + 20 =$ _____

6. $43 + 20 + 5 =$ _____

7. $23 + 30 =$ _____

8. $23 + 30 + 6 =$ _____

9. $33 + 20 + 5 =$ _____

10. $53 + 30 + 8 =$ _____

11. $38 + 24 =$ _____

12. $26 + 15 =$ _____

13. $83 + 16 =$ _____

14. $39 + 12 =$ _____

15. $42 + 35 =$ _____

16. $27 + 45 =$ _____

17. $36 + 18 =$ _____

18. $52 + 27 =$ _____

19. $54 + 35 =$ _____

20. $82 + 18 =$ _____

Adding from the Front End

1. 3 tens + 4 = _____

2. 4 tens + 8 = _____

3. 7 tens + 8 = _____

4. 5 tens + 2 = _____

5. 3 tens + 12 = _____

6. 5 tens + 15 = _____

7. 6 tens + 13 = _____

8. 4 tens + 6 = _____

9. 2 tens + 14 = _____

10. 1 ten + 11 = _____

11. 40 + 20 + 6 + 2 = _____

12. 30 + 20 + 5 + 4 = _____

13. 40 + 20 + 3 + 5 = _____

14. 60 + 20 + 5 + 2 = _____

15. 36 + 28 = _____

16. 45 + 25 = _____

17. 36 + 29 = _____

18. 84 + 15 = _____

19. 43 + 25 = _____

20. 46 + 53 = _____

Subtracting Multiples of Ten

1. 4 tens – 1 ten = _____

2. 8 tens – 3 tens = _____

3. 5 tens – 3 tens = _____

4. 8 tens – 2 tens = _____

5. 70 – 20 = _____

6. 30 – 20 = _____

7. 50 – 10 = _____

8. 80 – 40 = _____

9. 600 – 200 = _____

10. 400 – 200 = _____

11. 900 – 800 = _____

12. 1000 – 500 = _____

13. 1300 – 800 = _____

14. 1200 – 400 = _____

15. 600 – 300 = _____

16. 1100 – 1000 = _____

17. 900 – 500 = _____

18. 1800 – 900 = _____

19. 1500 – 900 = _____

20. 1400 – 600 = _____

Subtracting a Multiple of Ten from a Number

1. 34 − 1 ten = _____

2. 27 − 1 ten = _____

3. 84 − 1 ten = _____

4. 93 − 1 ten = _____

5. 56 − 2 tens = _____

6. 85 − 2 tens = _____

7. 63 − 10 = _____

8. 75 − 10 = _____

9. 54 − 10 = _____

10. 68 − 10 = _____

11. 85 − 10 − 10 = _____

12. 63 − 10 − 10 = _____

13. 47 − 10 − 10 = _____

14. 53 − 10 − 10 = _____

15. 56 − 20 = _____

16. 93 − 20 = _____

17. 85 − 40 = _____

18. 67 − 30 = _____

19. 98 − 30 = _____

20. 76 − 40 = _____

Subtracting a Number Ending in 9

1. $86 - 10 + 1 =$ _____

2. $47 - 10 + 1 =$ _____

3. $58 - 10 + 1 =$ _____

4. $93 - 10 + 1 =$ _____

5. $58 - 20 + 1 =$ _____

6. $67 - 20 + 1 =$ _____

7. $86 - 30 + 1 =$ _____

8. $76 - 30 + 1 =$ _____

9. $43 - 9 =$ _____

10. $62 - 9 =$ _____

11. $58 - 9 =$ _____

12. $27 - 9 =$ _____

13. $43 - 19 =$ _____

14. $63 - 19 =$ _____

15. $84 - 19 =$ _____

16. $57 - 19 =$ _____

17. $65 - 29 =$ _____

18. $84 - 39 =$ _____

19. $92 - 39 =$ _____

20. $58 - 29 =$ _____

Subtracting Numbers with Like Endings

1. $58 - 8 =$ _____

2. $43 - 3 =$ _____

3. $62 - 2 =$ _____

4. $59 - 9 =$ _____

5. $63 - 3 =$ _____

6. $95 - 5 =$ _____

7. $82 - 12 =$ _____

8. $73 - 13 =$ _____

9. $94 - 14 =$ _____

10. $62 - 12 =$ _____

11. $85 - 25 =$ _____

12. $68 - 28 =$ _____

13. $43 - 13 =$ _____

14. $97 - 37 =$ _____

15. $74 - 34 =$ _____

16. $52 - 32 =$ _____

17. $57 - 17 =$ _____

18. $76 - 26 =$ _____

19. $83 - 43 =$ _____

20. $96 - 56 =$ _____

ANSWER KEY FOR POWER BUILDERS

POWER BUILDER 1 — LESSONS 1–2

Counting On

1.
7 +2 9	5 +3 8	8 +1 9	4 +2 6	8 +3 11	9 +1 10	3 +6 9	2 +5 7

2.
3 +7 10	4 +1 5	6 +2 8	2 +9 11	1 +5 6	3 +4 7	6 +1 7	8 +2 10

3.
2 +4 6	7 +1 8	5 +2 7	1 +8 9	9 +3 12	6 +3 9	3 +8 11	1 +9 10

4.
2 +7 9	3 +9 12	4 +3 7	2 +8 10	3 +5 8	7 +3 10	9 +2 11	5 +1 6

POWER BUILDER 2 — LESSONS 3–5

Using Doubles

1.
6 +6 12	8 +7 15	5 +6 11	9 +7 16	4 +4 8	6 +8 14	6 +4 10	8 +9 17

2.
4 +5 9	6 +7 13	9 +8 17	3 +4 7	7 +7 14	5 +7 12	9 +9 18	3 +3 6

3.
7 +8 15	8 +9 17	7 +5 12	7 +9 16	6 +6 12	8 +6 14	4 +6 10	9 +8 17

4.
4 +3 7	5 +5 10	7 +6 13	3 +3 6	5 +7 12	8 +8 16	3 +5 8	5 +4 9

POWER BUILDER 3 — LESSONS 6–8

Making Ten and Adding with Ten

1.
4 +6 10	10 +3 13	9 +5 14	6 +10 16	7 +3 10	8 +5 13	4 +9 13	2 +8 10

2.
9 +6 15	1 +9 10	8 +4 12	10 +5 15	6 +4 10	2 +10 12	3 +8 11	10 +4 14

3.
3 +7 10	5 +8 13	7 +10 17	5 +9 14	8 +2 10	10 +6 16	9 +4 13	10 +3 13

4.
10 +2 12	9 +3 12	8 +3 11	5 +10 15	4 +8 12	5 +5 10	3 +9 12	9 +1 10

POWER BUILDER 4 — LESSONS 1–9

Basic Facts in Addition

1.
8 +5 13	9 +6 15	2 +1 3	3 +6 9	3 +3 6	8 +9 17	2 +4 6	3 +4 7

2.
2 +8 10	3 +1 4	7 +9 16	8 +3 11	2 +6 8	9 +9 18	4 +9 13	2 +9 11

3.
6 +3 9	8 +6 14	8 +4 12	6 +8 14	1 +2 3	1 +6 7	5 +9 14	6 +5 11

4.
2 +2 4	8 +2 10	9 +4 13	1 +3 4	4 +5 9	4 +7 11	5 +2 7	3 +7 10

5.
4 +3 7	5 +7 12	7 +1 8	1 +9 10	2 +5 7	3 +8 11	5 +6 11	1 +5 6

110   MENTAL MATH IN THE PRIMARY GRADES

POWER BUILDER 9 — LESSON 16

Using "Make Ten" Combinations

1.

13 −9	15 −8	17 −9	13 −7	14 −8	12 −9	15 −7	12 −8
4	7	8	6	6	3	8	4

2.

13 −8	15 −9	12 −7	16 −9	14 −7	11 −8	10 −7	18 −9
5	6	5	7	7	3	3	9

3.

16 −8	12 −8	14 −9	17 −9	11 −7	16 −7	12 −9	14 −8
8	4	5	8	4	9	3	6

4.

16 −8	18 −9	11 −9	15 −9	17 −8	16 −7	14 −6	16 −9
8	9	2	6	9	9	8	7

POWER BUILDER 10 — LESSONS 10–18

Basic Facts in Subtraction

1.

6 −5	7 −6	8 −7	9 −2	13 −5	7 −4	15 −7	14 −7
1	1	1	7	8	3	8	7

2.

12 −4	10 −6	3 −1	14 −8	14 −6	4 −2	10 −8	12 −7
8	4	2	6	8	2	2	5

3.

9 −6	16 −7	10 −4	13 −4	8 −1	9 −4	12 −3	10 −2
3	9	6	9	7	5	9	8

4.

10 −3	18 −9	9 −1	14 −9	12 −8	15 −9	6 −4	3 −2
7	9	8	5	4	6	2	1

5.

15 −8	10 −5	11 −3	8 −5	17 −9	11 −2	9 −3	11 −6
7	5	8	3	8	9	6	5

POWER BUILDER 11 — LESSONS 10–18

Basic Facts in Subtraction

1.

8 −3	4 −1	5 −1	9 −8	6 −2	6 −1	12 −9	7 −2
5	3	4	1	4	5	3	5

2.

4 −3	11 −7	5 −4	9 −5	12 −6	11 −4	13 −6	8 −2
1	4	1	4	6	7	7	6

3.

10 −7	16 −8	13 −8	10 −1	14 −5	7 −3	11 −9	13 −7
3	8	5	9	9	4	2	6

4.

5 −2	17 −8	9 −7	5 −3	12 −5	11 −5	7 −1	6 −3
3	9	2	2	7	6	6	3

5.

15 −6	8 −4	8 −6	13 −9	11 −8	7 −5	16 −9	10 −9
9	4	2	4	3	2	7	1

POWER BUILDER 12 — LESSON 28

Adding Multiples of Ten

1. 40 + 50 = 90
2. 30 + 10 = 40
3. 20 + 70 = 90
4. 80 + 30 = 110
5. 40 + 60 = 100
6. 90 + 20 = 110
7. 50 + 50 = 100
8. 30 + 80 = 110
9. 10 + 70 = 80
10. 70 + 50 = 120
11. 90 + 50 = 140
12. 10 + 90 = 100
13. 40 + 20 = 60
14. 20 + 80 = 100
15. 90 + 40 = 130
16. 60 + 50 = 110
17. 30 + 20 + 10 = 60
18. 20 + 20 + 50 = 90
19. 50 + 40 + 20 = 110
20. 10 + 30 + 90 = 130

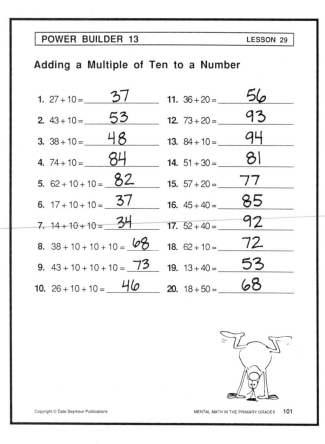

POWER BUILDER 13 LESSON 29

Adding a Multiple of Ten to a Number

1. 27 + 10 = __37__
2. 43 + 10 = __53__
3. 38 + 10 = __48__
4. 74 + 10 = __84__
5. 62 + 10 + 10 = __82__
6. 17 + 10 + 10 = __37__
7. 14 + 10 + 10 = __34__
8. 38 + 10 + 10 + 10 = __68__
9. 43 + 10 + 10 + 10 = __73__
10. 26 + 10 + 10 = __46__

11. 36 + 20 = __56__
12. 73 + 20 = __93__
13. 84 + 10 = __94__
14. 51 + 30 = __81__
15. 57 + 20 = __77__
16. 45 + 40 = __85__
17. 52 + 40 = __92__
18. 62 + 10 = __72__
19. 13 + 40 = __53__
20. 18 + 50 = __68__

POWER BUILDER 14 LESSON 30

Adding a Number Ending in 9

1. 34 + 9 = __43__
2. 82 + 9 = __91__
3. 15 + 9 = __24__
4. 23 + 9 = __32__
5. 26 + 9 = __35__
6. 43 + 9 = __52__
7. 38 + 19 = __57__
8. 52 + 19 = __71__
9. 65 + 19 = __84__
10. 74 + 19 = __93__

11. 38 + 29 = __67__
12. 43 + 39 = __82__
13. 52 + 29 = __81__
14. 26 + 29 = __55__
15. 19 + 49 = __68__
16. 38 + 39 = __77__
17. 51 + 39 = __90__
18. 62 + 19 = __81__
19. 82 + 19 = __101__
20. 43 + 29 = __72__

POWER BUILDER 15 LESSON 31

Adding by Expanding the Second Addend

1. 53 + 30 = __83__
2. 53 + 30 + 2 = __85__
3. 84 + 10 = __94__
4. 84 + 10 + 7 = __101__
5. 43 + 20 = __63__
6. 43 + 20 + 5 = __68__
7. 23 + 30 = __53__
8. 23 + 30 + 6 = __59__
9. 33 + 20 + 5 = __58__
10. 53 + 30 + 8 = __91__

11. 38 + 24 = __62__
12. 26 + 15 = __41__
13. 83 + 16 = __99__
14. 39 + 12 = __51__
15. 42 + 35 = __77__
16. 27 + 45 = __72__
17. 36 + 18 = __54__
18. 52 + 27 = __79__
19. 54 + 35 = __89__
20. 82 + 18 = __100__

POWER BUILDER 16 LESSON 32

Adding from the Front End

1. 3 tens + 4 = __34__
2. 4 tens + 8 = __48__
3. 7 tens + 8 = __78__
4. 5 tens + 2 = __52__
5. 3 tens + 12 = __42__
6. 5 tens + 15 = __65__
7. 6 tens + 13 = __73__
8. 4 tens + 6 = __46__
9. 2 tens + 14 = __34__
10. 1 ten + 11 = __21__

11. 40 + 20 + 6 + 2 = __68__
12. 30 + 20 + 5 + 4 = __59__
13. 40 + 20 + 3 + 5 = __68__
14. 60 + 20 + 5 + 2 = __87__
15. 36 + 28 = __64__
16. 45 + 25 = __70__
17. 36 + 29 = __65__
18. 84 + 15 = __99__
19. 43 + 25 = __68__
20. 46 + 53 = __99__

POWER BUILDER 17 LESSON 33

Subtracting Multiples of Ten

1. 4 tens – 1 ten = __30__
2. 8 tens – 3 tens = __50__
3. 5 tens – 3 tens = __20__
4. 8 tens – 2 tens = __60__
5. 70 – 20 = __50__
6. 30 – 20 = __10__
7. 50 – 10 = __40__
8. 80 – 40 = __40__
9. 600 – 200 = __400__
10. 400 – 200 = __200__
11. 900 – 800 = __100__
12. 1000 – 500 = __500__
13. 1300 – 800 = __500__
14. 1200 – 400 = __800__
15. 600 – 300 = __300__
16. 1100 – 1000 = __100__
17. 900 – 500 = __400__
18. 1800 – 900 = __900__
19. 1500 – 900 = __600__
20. 1400 – 600 = __800__

POWER BUILDER 18 LESSON 34

Subtracting a Multiple of Ten from a Number

1. 34 – 1 ten = __24__
2. 27 – 1 ten = __17__
3. 84 – 1 ten = __74__
4. 93 – 1 ten = __83__
5. 56 – 2 tens = __36__
6. 85 – 2 tens = __65__
7. 63 – 10 = __53__
8. 75 – 10 = __65__
9. 54 – 10 = __44__
10. 68 – 10 = __58__
11. 85 – 10 – 10 = __65__
12. 63 – 10 – 10 = __43__
13. 47 – 10 – 10 = __27__
14. 53 – 10 – 10 = __33__
15. 56 – 20 = __36__
16. 93 – 20 = __73__
17. 85 – 40 = __45__
18. 67 – 30 = __37__
19. 98 – 30 = __68__
20. 76 – 40 = __36__

POWER BUILDER 19 LESSON 35

Subtracting a Number Ending in 9

1. 86 – 10 + 1 = __77__
2. 47 – 10 + 1 = __38__
3. 58 – 10 + 1 = __49__
4. 93 – 10 + 1 = __84__
5. 58 – 20 + 1 = __39__
6. 67 – 20 + 1 = __48__
7. 86 – 30 + 1 = __57__
8. 76 – 30 + 1 = __47__
9. 43 – 9 = __34__
10. 62 – 9 = __53__
11. 58 – 9 = __49__
12. 27 – 9 = __18__
13. 43 – 19 = __24__
14. 63 – 19 = __44__
15. 84 – 19 = __65__
16. 57 – 19 = __38__
17. 65 – 29 = __36__
18. 84 – 39 = __45__
19. 92 – 39 = __53__
20. 58 – 29 = __29__

POWER BUILDER 20 LESSON 36

Subtracting Numbers with Like Endings

1. 58 – 8 = __50__
2. 43 – 3 = __40__
3. 62 – 2 = __60__
4. 59 – 9 = __50__
5. 63 – 3 = __60__
6. 95 – 5 = __90__
7. 82 – 12 = __70__
8. 73 – 13 = __60__
9. 94 – 14 = __80__
10. 62 – 12 = __50__
11. 85 – 25 = __60__
12. 68 – 28 = __40__
13. 43 – 13 = __30__
14. 97 – 37 = __60__
15. 74 – 34 = __40__
16. 52 – 32 = __20__
17. 57 – 17 = __40__
18. 76 – 26 = __50__
19. 83 – 43 = __40__
20. 96 – 56 = __40__

THE 100 CHART

0	1	2	3	4	5	6	7	8	9
10	11	12	13	14	15	16	17	18	19
20	21	22	23	24	25	26	27	28	29
30	31	32	33	34	35	36	37	38	39
40	41	42	43	44	45	46	47	48	49
50	51	52	53	54	55	56	57	58	59
60	61	62	63	64	65	66	67	68	69
70	71	72	73	74	75	76	77	78	79
80	81	82	83	84	85	86	87	88	89
90	91	92	93	94	95	96	97	98	99

FOUR 100 CHARTS

0	1	2	3	4	5	6	7	8	9
10	11	12	13	14	15	16	17	18	19
20	21	22	23	24	25	26	27	28	29
30	31	32	33	34	35	36	37	38	39
40	41	42	43	44	45	46	47	48	49
50	51	52	53	54	55	56	57	58	59
60	61	62	63	64	65	66	67	68	69
70	71	72	73	74	75	76	77	78	79
80	81	82	83	84	85	86	87	88	89
90	91	92	93	94	95	96	97	98	99

0	1	2	3	4	5	6	7	8	9
10	11	12	13	14	15	16	17	18	19
20	21	22	23	24	25	26	27	28	29
30	31	32	33	34	35	36	37	38	39
40	41	42	43	44	45	46	47	48	49
50	51	52	53	54	55	56	57	58	59
60	61	62	63	64	65	66	67	68	69
70	71	72	73	74	75	76	77	78	79
80	81	82	83	84	85	86	87	88	89
90	91	92	93	94	95	96	97	98	99

0	1	2	3	4	5	6	7	8	9
10	11	12	13	14	15	16	17	18	19
20	21	22	23	24	25	26	27	28	29
30	31	32	33	34	35	36	37	38	39
40	41	42	43	44	45	46	47	48	49
50	51	52	53	54	55	56	57	58	59
60	61	62	63	64	65	66	67	68	69
70	71	72	73	74	75	76	77	78	79
80	81	82	83	84	85	86	87	88	89
90	91	92	93	94	95	96	97	98	99

0	1	2	3	4	5	6	7	8	9
10	11	12	13	14	15	16	17	18	19
20	21	22	23	24	25	26	27	28	29
30	31	32	33	34	35	36	37	38	39
40	41	42	43	44	45	46	47	48	49
50	51	52	53	54	55	56	57	58	59
60	61	62	63	64	65	66	67	68	69
70	71	72	73	74	75	76	77	78	79
80	81	82	83	84	85	86	87	88	89
90	91	92	93	94	95	96	97	98	99

MASTER FOR TAGBOARD BASE TEN BLOCKS

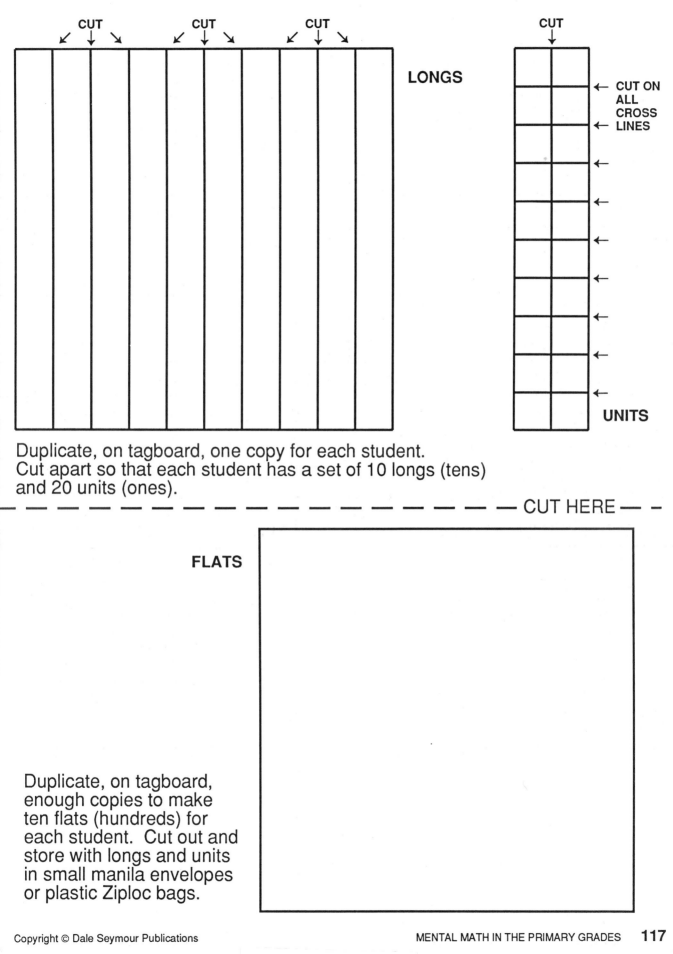

LONGS

CUT   CUT   CUT

CUT

UNITS

← CUT ON ALL CROSS LINES

Duplicate, on tagboard, one copy for each student.
Cut apart so that each student has a set of 10 longs (tens)
and 20 units (ones).

— CUT HERE — —

FLATS

Duplicate, on tagboard,
enough copies to make
ten flats (hundreds) for
each student. Cut out and
store with longs and units
in small manila envelopes
or plastic Ziploc bags.

3 1511 00206 2627